THE EMOTIONALLY
TROUBLED CHILD

THE EMOTIONALLY TROUBLED CHILD

A Guide for Parents and Teachers in the Early Recognition of Mental and Nervous Disorders in Children

By

ROBERT L. MASON, JR. Ed. D.
Counseling Psychologist, University Health Service
Assistant Professor of Education
University of Georgia
Athens, Georgia

BERT O. RICHMOND, Ed. D.
Coordinator, School Psychology Program
Co-director, Child Guidance Center
Professor of Education
University of Georgia
Athens, Georgia

LUCIEN B. FLEURANT, M.D.
Chief, Mental Health Division
Assistant Director, University Health Service
University of Georgia
Athens, Georgia

CHARLES C THOMAS · PUBLISHER
Springfield · Illinois · U.S.A.

Published and Distributed Throughout the World by

CHARLES C THOMAS • PUBLISHER

BANNERSTONE HOUSE

301-327 East Lawrence Avenue, Springfield, Illinois, U.S.A.

© *1976, by* CHARLES C THOMAS • PUBLISHER

ISBN 0-398-03557-1

Library of Congress Catalog Card Number: 76-1930

With THOMAS BOOKS *careful attention is given to all details of
manufacturing and design. It is the Publisher's desire to present
books that are satisfactory as to their physical qualities and artistic
possibilities and appropriate for their particular use.* THOMAS
BOOKS *will be true to those laws of quality that assure a good
name and good will.*

Printed in the United States of America

N-11

Library of Congress Cataloging in Publication Data

Mason, Robert Lee.
    The emotionally troubled child.

    Bibliography: p.
    Includes index.
    1. Mentally ill children. 2. Problem children. I. Richmond, Bert O.,
joint author. II. Fleurant, Lucien B., joint author. III. Title. [DNLM:
1. Affective disturbances—In infancy and childhood. 2. Mental disorders—In infancy and childhood. WS350 M411e]
RJ499.M33   618.9'28'9   79-1930
ISBN 0-398-03557-1

DEDICATION

A̲S MILLIONS OF STUDENTS can attest, there are literally thousands of teachers, young and old, male and female, possessing the qualities, inherent or acquired, which have enabled them to touch the lives of students in ways never measured by performance in class or by standardized tests. To this select group of teachers this book is dedicated for it is in truth such individuals as these who have made it possible to refer to teaching as the greatest profession in the world and mean it.

This book is also dedicated to the many conscientious and concerned parents who, despite their fears and doubts about being good parents, manage to do a most commendable job.

And last but not least, this book is dedicated to Bonnie, Debbie, Lianne, Lucy, Mike, Ricky and Steve, whom we believe to be fairly representative of children everywhere.

the authors

PROLOGUE

As early as the first grade Ms. Thomas, Jena's teacher, had begun to suspect that all was not well with Jena.

One of the most intelligent children in her grade, she often had difficulty doing simple tasks which other children in the class performed with ease. For example, while making Christmas decorations or helping with some other class project she would often find it difficult to complete the work. Instead, she would retire to her seat where she would sit for long periods of time, often crying. Ms. Thomas's efforts to comfort and reassure Jena met with little visible response.

Ms. Thomas made several attempts to convey to Jena's parents her concern regarding Jena's behavior. Jena's mother, like most mothers, wanted her children to do well in school and like many parents rejected any suggestion that Jena might need professional help. A strict disciplinarian who accepted nothing less than perfection from her children, she usually responded by forcing Jena to work for long periods of time after school on the class assignments she had been unable to complete during the day.

In the second grade Jena's behavior remained pretty much unchanged. Still making top grades, she would now cry frequently over minor incidents. Despite her efforts to be a part of the class, due largely to her mother's insistence, she seemed unable to fit in or relate to the other children. A quiet and submissive child, never considered a disciplinary problem, she spent a large portion of her time alone both at home and at school.

Unfortunately, her second grade teacher did not possess the sensitivity and patience of Ms. Thomas. After minimal efforts to work with Jena she would either ignore her or banish her to a corner of the room where Jena would either cry or read alone. When she did cry, her new teacher's usual response was to get angry and send a note home to her parents informing them of Jena's behavior.

By this time, frustrated and tired of such reports, Jena's parents had resorted to spanking whenever she brought home a note informing them that Jena had been crying again. Hoping to avoid such punishment, which was usually meted out several times each week, Jena soon learned to cry less, but withdrew even more into herself and her books. When she would arrive at home in the afternoon she would go to her room where, all by herself, she would study or listen to music for long periods of time.

While maintaining one of the highest scholastic averages in school, Jena had, by age fifteen, become very interested in church and other religious activities. For the most part a passive participant, religion had become a major force in her thinking.

Having learned to keep most of her concerns to herself, Jena had acquired the reputation of a good, hardworking and diligent student and daughter who would someday make her mark in the world. It was therefore with some surprise that Ms. Gray, Jena's eleventh grade home room teacher, agreed, at Jena's request, to talk with her after school. Although she had learned to view Jena as a rather quiet and serious person prone to rumination and introspection, she was not prepared to hear Jena say that she was terribly depressed. Feeling that she could no longer cope with her despondent moods and the demands placed on her at school and at home, Jena said that she was thinking of killing herself.

Ms. Gray, a devoutly religious person herself and unprepared to cope with such a startling revelation, encouraged Jena to pray more and to trust in God with the assurance that he would help her. A very kind and caring person, Ms. Gray then asked Jena's permission to talk with her parents. The meeting arranged, Jena's parents again elected to ignore their daughter's plight, insisting that Jena was just a moody person whose mood would improve in the next few days after her quarterly exams were over.

In her senior year Jena once again, in an attempt to express her need for some sort of relief, approached her school principal and indicated in no uncertain terms her feelings that she needed some kind of help. Having checked several books on mental illness out of the library, Jena was convinced that she was about to go crazy unless some sort of help was forthcoming.

The principal, a close friend of the family and a golfing companion of her father, attempted to reassure Jena that she was not going crazy but was instead overreacting to the stresses to which most young people are exposed. He assured her that once school was out she would snap back and have a good vacation.

One week later Jean's father was asked by the school principal to come to his office. Interrupted in the middle of a business meeting, Jena's father, disturbed by the urgency in the principal's voice, agreed to come immediately. Shocked by the dazed and frightened expression on his daughter's face as she glanced furtively about the counselor's office where she now sat, he was informed that Jena had been going through the halls at lunchtime telling students and teachers that she was the Virgin Mary's daughter and had been sent to warn them of some terrible disaster which was about to occur.

Convinced by now that his daughter was on some kind of drug, Jena's father, upon reaching home, ushered her into his combination study and business office. Demanding that she explain why she had done this to her parents who had done so much for her, he slapped her across the face several times when she did not answer. When she denied the use of any drugs he locked her in her bedroom and told her she could come out when she was ready to tell the truth.

Later that evening when Jena began to scream and talk incoherently, trying to jump out of her second story bedroom window, a doctor was summoned. Taken to the hospital in an ambulance where she had to be strapped down after she had tried to jump out of the moving vehicle, she was later transferred to a mental hospital where she remained for the next six months.

The week following her admission to the hospital, her school announced that she had made the highest average in her graduating class. Two and one-half years after her initial admission to the hospital Jena has been readmitted on two other occasions. In the intervals between hospitalizations, she was seen regularly by a psychiatrist on an outpatient basis.

FOREWORD

THE PROFESSIONAL literature about emotional disturbances in children is extensive and usually written in a very technical manner. Parents, teachers, school counselors, and the general lay public are often bewildered and confused by the frequency and apparent complexity of the terms. In my opinion Robert Mason, Jr., Ed.D., Bert Richmond, Ed.D., and Lucien B. Fleurant, M.D. have performed a useful, constructive public service in the preparation of this guide, "The Emotionally Troubled Child." They have designed their presentation with clinical vignettes, so that readers may obtain a general overview of troubled children and can identify specific examples of behavioral problems that are encountered in school and home.

It is evident that the study of normal and deviant behavior is becoming very complex in our country and in the world. Biochemical and other biological scientific discoveries of physiological processes (and possible psychopharmacological interventions) are appearing rapidly in the literature. Although longitudinal psychological studies seem to be disappearing, the observations about mother-child interactions, the concepts of parenting, the attempts to establish microanalytic observational techniques about human behavior are sophisticated and more and more relevant to the concerns of parents and teachers.

Although our own culture seems to be expanding aimlessly, with powerful trends toward multiethnic and multilingual patterns, elaborate cross-cultural research designs are enabling scientists to explore the impact of these changes on our children, too.

The authors have recognized the importance of excessive stress and genetic and constitutional deficits that limit and modify the child's capability to respond to stressful situations. Their case examples in preschool and the early years of life are excellent, and the wide range of examples of various problems should prove to be useful to their readers in their search for awareness of potential problems, the key to early identification and appropriate intervention.

ROBERT L. STUBBLEFIELD, M.D.
Medical Director and Administrator
Silver Hill Foundation
New Canaan, Connecticut

CONTENTS

THE EMOTIONALLY
TROUBLED CHILD

Chapter 1

INTRODUCTION

". . . and in a really dark night of the soul it is always three o'clock in the morning, day after day."[1]

F. SCOTT FITZGERALD

H OW DOES ONE RECOGNIZE and identify the emotionally troubled child? Of the many questions asked of psychologists and psychiatrists in meetings with parents and teachers no other question is raised with such frequency or intensity of interest.

Parents, in both public and private meetings with psychologists, ask, "How can we distinguish between behavior which is normal and behavior which might mean that our child is mentally ill?" In seminars, classrooms and consultations with educators, psychiatrists are bombarded with questions from teachers who want to know how they can identify the student who needs referral for psychiatric help. Even physicians, guidance counselors, social workers, nurses, school psychologists and other mental health workers often feel the need for assistance as they attempt to provide answers to these and similar questions from parents, teachers and children.

Despite this interest and search for answers from a sizeable number of parents, teachers and other professionals, Jena, as presented in the *Prologue* of this book, is a good example of our ignorance and neglect when it comes to those children suffering from emotional problems. Teachers, administrators, parents and others in positions of responsibility too often manage to ignore the many signals or cries for help until irreparable damage has been done or until the situation becomes so intolerable that it can no longer be endured by either the child or those around him.

Even teachers and parents who are sincerely interested in both the mental and physical as well as scholastic well-being of their students and children are often hampered in their efforts to help due to a lack of time or training necessary to provide help to those suffering from emotional problems.

3

This book is a response to requests for such information and assistance. It is written in the hope that it might in some way help to break through the omnipresent cloud of ignorance, confusion and insensitivity whenever and wherever mental illness rears its head. For those teachers, parents and others already interested in the prevention, recognition and treatment of mental illness in their children and students, it is hoped that the material will in some way provide the structure and guidelines necessary to make a difficult task less difficult.

Since there are already many excellent books dealing with theories and treatment of mental illness, this book will be concerned primarily with the problem of early recognition.

As a result of the pleas from parents and teachers for help in the recognition of emotional problems without having to wade through volumes of material written in medical or psychological jargon which they find difficult to follow, the authors have attempted to find ways to present pertinent information in the most readable fashion.

Teachers and parents have suggested that actual case studies are the simplest and most interesting way of communicating the information they desire. As a result of these suggestions this book is, for the most part, a book of cases selected from our clinical and teaching experiences which seem to be representative of the types of emotional problems most often experienced by children in the home and school.

While this book is largely the outcome of requests from teachers and parents, we have also undertaken this endeavor for the simple reason that we are convinced that mental illness is by far the major health problem in our schools, homes and communities today.

Most individuals have in some way experienced or witnessed the trauma of mental illness either in their own families or in those of neighbors or friends. While it may be said that no person is totally immune to the ravages of mental illness, authorities have become increasingly concerned in recent years by the number of children and adolescents suffering from emotional disorders.

While there has been a great hue and cry from the highest officials in government to the person on the street regarding the need for physical fitness, there has been no corresponding plea or emphasis regarding mental fitness in most homes and school programs.

This callousness or seeming lack of concern is especially difficult to understand when it is recognized that, of all the misfortunes suffered by mankind, none is more tragic or has such far-reaching repercussions for the victim and his family as mental illness.

While the loneliness, fear and confusion known only to those who have trod the pathways of mental illness is in itself tragedy enough, the tragedy is compounded by the lack of response on the part of our so-called sane population toward those so desperately in need of help and human compassion.

Mental health is still the stepchild whenever health care programs are discussed. Few seem to be concerned that equal consideration be given to mental health needs. Many parents, teachers and school officials still view mental health programs as frills and would be happy to dispense with all such programs despite the growing number of youngsters suffering from emotional disorders and the pain and suffering engendered by mental illness for millions.

From kindergarten to the university we are bombarded daily with facts and warnings about cancer as well as lung and heart diseases. For some strange reason these same officials will ignore pleas for mental health programs despite the indisputable fact that more individuals are suffering from emotional and nervous disorders than from all physical illnesses combined.

In addition to the pain suffered by the victim, the despair and agony within families and in the community as a product of mental illness is beyond measure. While the child afflicted with heart disease is cause for great concern, he is much more apt to live a *normal* life than is a sibling or classmate suffering from some serious emotional disorder. It is not uncommon for an emotionally troubled child to disrupt not only his immediate family, but quite often his distress and despair are communicated to the entire classroom.

On some occasions the more disruptive child is capable of keeping entire neighborhoods in turmoil.

While the victims of mental illness are often ostracized or stigmatized, or more often ignored, it is interesting to note the progress made in other areas in the field of technology and science.

In less than a century we have gone from the sands of Kitty Hawk to the moon and back. With an ever-increasing body of knowledge concerning distant planets and stars, man has by comparison made little progress in our understanding of those things closest to us—our emotions and relationships with other human beings.

Despite the advances made in recent years in many areas of science, the number of individuals needing mental health aid continues to stagger the imagination. While there are those who would argue that Jena is a rare and extreme example, such tragedies do occur and with much greater frequency than we like to admit. Admittedly, most emotionally-troubled children do not experience this much disruption in their lives or for so long a period of time; there are, however, large numbers who do, and millions more experience emotional problems of lesser intensity that are not so devastating. Nevertheless their problems are severe enough to interfere with their ability to function at a desirable or optimal level.

While we are primarily concerned here with the more personal aspects of mental illness suffered by Jena and countless others like her, we cannot ignore the suffering and problems encountered as a result of emotional problems on a larger social spectrum. While it is difficult to establish any definite cause and effect relationship in regard to many of the problems plaguing our society today, we would like to suggest a possible link between the increasing incidence of mental illness and the escalating number of behavioral problems evident in children throughout our society today.

While we would not be so presumptuous as to suggest that all behavioral problems either at home or in school are caused by those suffering from some form of emotional instabilty, it is very possible that many problems including those of discipline, learning, drugs, pregnancy, abortion, suicide, cheating, theft and even more serious crimes including rape and murder are in a significant number of cases the result of emotional problems or mental disturbances among young people.

In a recent newspaper article by Associated Press writer, Dolores Barclay, discussing the increase in violent crimes committed by juveniles, Leon Herman, administrator of the Goshen New York Center for Boys, is quoted as saying "These children are the debris of society in terms of the emotionally disturbed." In the same article Dr. David Abrahamsen, a psychoanalyst who has studied the nature of violence, is quoted as saying, "If you look beneath the pattern of violence you see a disturbance among these children—a cry for help. Since they do not get attention from their parents or friends, they try to get attention from killing."[2]

Unfortunately, and contrary to what many believe, mental illness does not go away if ignored as the child grows older. *Mentally ill children usually turn out to be mentally ill adults.*

Mental illness is almost never a sudden occurrence. Often viewed in adults as a drastic and sudden change in personality and ability to function, mental illness is more often than not a slow and gradual process with its origin somewhere in the earlier years. It almost never strikes without first giving off many clues or danger signals over an extended period of time that something is wrong.

The immensity of the problem of mental illness in this country becomes apparent from even a cursory examination of statistics involving the number of individuals hospitalized or treated on an outpatient basis for psychological reasons. Conservative estimates indicate that one out of every ten people will at some time or other be treated for emotional problems. This does not include the large number of individuals who need psychiatric and neurological help but who, for various reasons, never obtain such help.

Dr. Alfred Freedman, former president of the American Psychiatric Association, has estimated that three out of four persons over fifteen years of age currently in need of psychiatric care do not receive it.[3] In a similar vein, neurologists know that for each child with epilepsy experiencing convulsions, there are many times this number who never experience a seizure and are therefore never diagnosed or treated for epilepsy. Most of these individuals, if treated with proper medication, could be spared years of needless suffering, both physical and emotional.

Some physicians estimate that more than half of their patients are suffering from psychological rather than physiological problems. In some cases the estimates are even higher.

While most individuals who smoke pot or drink alcohol are not mentally ill, the abuse of these drugs at all ages strongly suggests that other problems exist. While alcoholism and drug abuse have traditionally been viewed as adult problems, the trend in recent years indicates that alcohol and other drugs are now a matter of concern in the elementary and high school years.

Dr. Morris Chafetz, cited in a recent newspaper article by Karen Peterson as the government's number one alcohol abuse expert, says, "Cases of alcoholism among children 9 to 12 years old are becoming more and more frequent . . . Youngsters who become alcoholics have many other problems. Alcoholism may be their most crucial symptom, but still it is only a symptom of great personal trauma. Alcoholism is their plea for help."[4]

In the same article national statistics are cited revealing that, by the age of fourteen, seven out of ten young people have tasted alcohol. By the age of sixteen this number has risen to 87 percent. Of course most of them don't get hooked, but enough do to the point that Alcoholics Anonymous now sponsors twenty-five youth-oriented meetings compared to twelve one year ago. Five years ago there were none.[5]

Regarding the relationship between drugs and suicide among youths, Richard Seiden, a clinical psychologist at the University of California School of Public Health, is quoted as saying that suicide among young Americans is increasing by almost epidemic proportions and the use of illegal drugs is largely to blame. The rate during 1970 to 1972 jumped 92 percent from the period 1940 to 1969. Seiden concludes by saying for every suicide there are approximately eight to ten times as many suicide attempts.[6]

In a recent series of articles by Charles Seabrook, dealing with troubled children in one of our southern states, facts are cited to point out the critical situation as it now exists regarding mental illness among young people.

——Ten percent of all school-age children have emotional problems requiring psychiatric help.

——The number of boys, ages ten through fourteen, in mental hospitals has increased six-fold since 1950 while the number of boys in the age group has doubled.

——The number of young people, ages fifteen through twenty-four, in mental hospitals has risen 35 percent in the past decade. An additional 70 percent increase is predicted for the coming year (1975).

——Suicide is the second leading cause of death among college students. By the most generous estimates only 12 percent of those needing help will get mental health care.[7]

In a recent article in the *American Personal and Guidance Journal,* Robert Couchman quotes Michael Begab (1967) of the United States Public Health Service as saying that 1.5 American children in ten, up to the age of sixteen, suffer serious mental health problems. In Canada, more recent estimates placed the figure at 1 in 6.5 people.[8]

In still another article appearing in *Family Health,* Dr. Stuart M. Finch, Professor of Psychiatry and Chief of the Children's Psychiatric Service at the University of Michigan Medical School, is quoted by Warren and Rebecca Boroson as saying,

Mental and emotional disorders in children represent one of the largest unmet health needs in our country today. It is estimated that several million youngsters—one out of every ten—need psychological or psychiatric help. The majority probably receive no help at all, either because their condition is not recognized or because there are insufficient mental health personnel to treat them.[9]

Aware that teachers have been criticized, maligned and blamed for everything from Johnny's inability to read to the moral decay of youth, the authors have chosen to address this book to teachers as well as parents for several reasons,

1. If it is true that mental illness is a gradual process with many danger signals usually transmitted over an extended period of

time prior to any acute or obvious breakdown of mental functioning, then it is the authors' contention that teachers as well as parents are in an excellent position to recognize and identify these warning symptoms before the problem becomes a major illness. Teachers have more exposure to children and young people than any other group of individuals with the possible exception of parents. Even here teachers often spend more time with the child than do the parents. Even when the parents are conscientious and dedicated they are frequently too involved and too close to the situation to make any evaluation of their child's need for professional help. In other cases they may be a major factor in the child's emotional difficulties. Some parents will also ignore signs that something is wrong with their child since, in their minds, recognition of the problem is equivalent to an admission that they have failed as parents.

2. Some states are now recommending that teachers have some training in the recognition and identification of problems which can affect the learning process.

3. The more obvious reason for addressing such a book to both teachers and parents is due to the simple and humane reason that, unless recognized and treated, a large number of emotionally troubled children may be doomed to years of emotional distress.

Whether teacher or parent, it is a sobering thought indeed to realize that in every group of one hundred children at least ten to fifteen may have serious emotional problems. Some mental health professionals suggest that the percentage may be much higher.

Even more sobering is the unnecessary waste of human energy and potential, for the truth is that a significant number of these individuals could lead normal and productive lives if proper treatment were begun early enough. Most authorities are quick to agree that mental problems are much more apt to respond favorably to treatment if recognized and if therapy is begun in the younger years. Despite the need for early diagnosis and treatment many students either drop out of school, graduate or enter adulthood without ever having any contact with a teacher, counselor or other professional trained to deal with emotional problems.

While there may be indifferent and incompetent teachers and parents with a sizable number having emotional problems themselves to the extent that they are unable to help or relate to children in a healthy fashion, most are capable and conscientious and have a sincere interest in the total well-being of their children or students.

Unlike school counselors or school psychologists who may be secluded in their offices and unaware of problems until called to their attention, parents and teachers are exposed to students in the home, the classroom, on the playground, in the lunchroom, at work and at play.

As a result of these daily and in-depth encounters with children, teachers and parents are in a much better position to spot behavior or other signs and symptoms indicating the child is experiencing emotional problems. They are also in a much better position to instigate corrective treatment.

In an effort to answer some of the questions raised about the ways in which mental illness may be manifested, it should be emphasized that the authors have no desire to make junior psychiatrists out of parents and teachers or to turn the home or classroom into group therapy sessions. We are instead concerned with providing parents and teachers with some basic infomation which will enable them to recognize behavior or attitudes in children which might alert them to the danger that emotional illness is already existent or to be expected in the future unless some sort of intervention is attempted.

While it is believed that most teachers and many parents have had some exposure to behavioral or mental disorders either through direct experience or through books, it is assumed that most teachers and parents have not had any intensive study in the recognition of psychopathology.

Although there are many capable and well-qualified school psychologists and counselors, many of them also do not have any training or experience in working with the more seriously disturbed child. Writing in a recent issue of a journal for school counselors Robert Couchman says,

Despite the myths that are propagated in counselor education programs, the majority of moderately and severely disturbed children and young people are not receiving intensive mental health care. They are sitting in overcroweded classrooms and being cared for by teachers untrained in the methods of mental health treatment. In most cases the teacher's only accessible resource is a school counselor who, alas, is also untrained in treating troubled children and young people.[10]

In attempting to communicate to interested parents and teachers information which might be of value to them in recognizing the child plagued with emotional problems it was decided, for the sake of discussion, to divide the cases, based on age and grade in school, into three separate groups as follows: (1) preschool and primary grades, (2) middle grades and (3) adolescence.

We have attempted to select cases on a continuum from the mildly troubled to the more seriously disturbed individual who will in some instances need hospitalization. We have also attempted to select cases in which the need for mental health or medical care may not be so obvious. For example, it is obvious that anyone having a seizure or convulsion in class should be receiving medical care. Likewise, the student who is so out of contact with reality that he or she is no longer able to perform simple tasks is also obviously in need of help. While some of the cases discussed will involve extreme behavior, the emphasis will be on those cases in which emotional problems are manifested in more subtle ways.

For example, it is not always the boisterous or disruptive student who needs help the most. It may well be that the quiet, obedient, compliant and well-mannered child who never gives the teacher any trouble is in greater need of help than the former.

Although the authors are convinced that a definite need exists for such a book as this, they are also aware of the problems and difficulties involved in the recognition of emotional disorders. Even mental health professionals with years of training and experience are often confused and uncertain in the diagnosis of certain problems. This lack of any sure-fire method of diagnosis and prognosis, is, among other things, one of the reasons why patients are released from mental hospitals and prisons and pronounced ready to resume their place in society only to relapse shortly thereafter or, in some cases, to commit some terrible crime again.

The reader should be cognizant of the many difficulties encountered in attempts to categorize individuals on the basis of behavior or attitudes and is therefore cautioned against the tendency to attach any label to any individual on the basis of any one or a combination of symptoms to be discussed in the following cases. A more comprehensive psychological or medical history may be required and is recommended whenever the prospect of mental illness is present.

Indeed it is not our purpose to attach any particular label to any individual. At the same time it is hoped that the presence of certain signs or symptoms discussed in the following pages will alert the reader to the possibility that the student may be experiencing psychological problems. If there is reason to suspect severe emotional problems, then referral to a mental health professional capable of evaluating psychological problems will reduce greatly the chances of unnecessary grief and suffering for many.

While most of us are not as articulate as F. Scott Fitzgerald who was quoted earlier and who knew something personally of the agonies endured by those plagued by the ups and downs of emotional illness, most individuals manage in some way to convey their distress. While not so poetic, the cases which follow will demonstrate the many ways students and children communicate their concerns about their mental condition.

Chapter 2

PRESCHOOL AND PRIMARY GRADES

IT IS UNUSUAL for a child to be referred for psychological or emotional problems prior to entry to school unless his behavior or circumstances are very severe. As examples, we have cases of child abuse which are more numerous than social and medical agencies are ever able to detect wherein the child is likely to experience severe emotional as well as physical stress. There is also the child who is autistic or who has suffered organic trauma and may be in obvious need of supportive therapy from all significant adults in his life. These children should be referred for professional psychological services, not only for the child but to aid parents in coping with the situation.

However, with the increase in Head Start Programs, day care centers, nursery schools and other community and governmental programs for young children, the very young child is often under the care of teachers and paraprofessionals outside of his home environment. The observant child care worker is often heard to express concern that a three or four-year-old is not able to fit in with a group of his peers. She may realize that the child has already established some patterns of behavior and social interaction that may lead to later emotional stress.

Although the child of three or four is just beginning the process of self-identification in relationships with peers, he has acquired a personality pattern based on his previous experiences. Children this age vary widely in the amount of nurturance that they require or will accept, in the causes and extent of their crying, in their degree of aggressiveness or submissiveness, and in other important ways.

Some children of this age will leave their parents readily to stay with a friendly child care worker whereas others will scream and kick or even refuse to leave their parents. Some children will fight to take toys from another child and some will give up a desired toy readily. Some preschoolers prefer the association of other children and some appear comfortable only when they are near the teacher. One little four-year-old boy sat down to his first meal in a Head Start summer program and began to push food into his mouth with both hands, completely ignoring the use of spoon and fork and apparently unaware that other children and the teachers were eating their food in a different manner. A visit to his severely deprived home environment revealed that he had never had any experience in eating with silverware.

The three to four-year-old child may also vary considerably in language skills, toilet training habits, cleanliness, willingness to take risks and other behavioral characteristics that relate to his later socialization skills and emotional flexibility. Thus, the child of three or four becomes the child of five or six who must enter some kind of school experience and the child of seven or eight who must continue to adapt to the increasing complexities of a world and social order in which he plays a dependent role.

Child guidance centers find an increasing number of young preschool children being referred for their services. This is perhaps a positive indication that both parents and professional workers are more sensitive to the needs of the young child. Kindergarten and early primary grade teachers are also expressing a greater awareness that the child from five to eight does indeed undergo various forms of emotional stress and may benefit from a more empathetic grasp of his problems and a more positive management of his home and school environment. Often, the child of this age is as much, if not more, in need of understanding and therapeutic treatment than is the more commonly recognized troubled teen-ager whom we will discuss in later sections.

Indeed, the proper therapeutic intervention in these early years may be necessary if we are to decrease the incidence and severity of personal and social maladjustment in adolescence and adulthood.

This section of the book that follows reports selected cases of children up to eight years old who have been referred by parents, teachers or concerned professional workers for psychological diagnosis and treatment. Although these cases do not describe all the kinds of stresses to which this age group is subject, they do illustrate some common problems of children.

It is anticipated that these cases may also serve to acquaint parents and teachers with some real-life examples of a troubled child. Hopefully it will alert them to recognize symptoms of emotional stress and give them the courage to dare to be involved with helping children grow in emotional strength.

Although not all of us can function as professional mental health workers, we can all realize that mental health is a cooperative venture at least as significant as classroom learning of academic subjects. Emotional health is a developmental process that begins at birth and continues whether we ignore it or aid it.

Thus, the conscientious parent and teacher realize that they are involved in the child's mental health and will strive to contribute to this mental health development in a positive manner.

Pepper

Pepper, the seven-year-old son of migrant farm workers, entered the first grade three weeks after school had started. His oldest sister, Billie, accompanied him to school and explained to the principal that Pepper had never been to school before because some doctor had told his parents several years earlier that he was retarded and would never be able to keep up with the other children in school. Agreeing with the doctor that Pepper was not too bright, his parents had not bothered to enroll him in the first grade the year before. It was only at Billie's insistence that they agreed to let him try the first grade five months after his seventh birthday.

The principal learned in talking with Billie that Pepper had in the last year learned to write his first name but still could not spell his last name. He had not learned to talk until he was three and still had a vocabulary much smaller than one would expect of a seven-year-old. He still needed help in going to the bathroom or dressing himself for the day. He never seemed to have much interest in doing anything with his five brothers and sisters or with other children where he lived. Billie admitted, however, that he seldom had a chance to get to know other children very well as they moved several times each year.

She also disclosed that they were not only very poor, sometimes going without a decent meal for several days, but also that her parents fought constantly, verbally and physically. On several occasions Pepper had seen his mother hit his father with a board or threaten him with a knife. His father also kept a pistol in the house and often threatened both his wife and children by waving the pistol when angry. On several occasions he had shot holes in the floor and ceiling although he had never hit anyone.

In his first month of school Pepper sat quietly at his desk most of the time. He seldom completed the tasks given him to do and usually seemed not to understand the directions even when Ms. Bell went to great lengths to explain them. He was still afraid to go to the bathroom alone and refused to go unless someone went with him. When through using the bathroom he would have to have someone help him pull his trousers back up and fasten his belt.

On the school ground he never played with the other children and usually sat alone with no interest in what was going on around him. Both inside and outside the classroom he seldom displayed any curiosity about anything. If he did play with toys occasionally, he did so alone and might play with the same toy for a long time. At other times his attention span seemed almost nonexistent. His physical movements were sluggish and his response to questions was usually "I don't know." His classmates soon began to tease him about being stupid and referred to him as Dummy. Ignoring their jeers and taunts, Pepper withdrew even more.

In his third month of school, Ms. Bell informed Pepper's mother that she agreed with the doctor who had said that Pepper was severely retarded and recommended that he be placed in a special school equipped to work with such youngsters. Insisting that they could not afford the special school, Pepper's parents instead placed him in a state hospital. Although it took several weeks before Pepper would cooperate enough to undergo testing, personality tests were administered which confirmed the psychiatrist's suspicions that Pepper had severe personality problems. Rather than being retarded as suspected earlier, it was learned that Pepper's intelligence was in the superior range.

Discussion

Unfortunately, emotional illness is sometimes misdiagnosed as mental retardation, which was until recently in our society tantamount to a life sentence in some institution, or at best a lifetime of just barely existing.

There are many problems which can result in the symptoms manifested by Pepper. Brain injury, tumors, malnutrition, lead poisoning, family problems and social and cultural deprivation are just a few of the medical or psychological difficulties which may lead one to suspect that the child is mentally retarded when in truth the child may be quite normal or above average in intelligence.

Whenever mental retardation is suspected, parents or teachers should see to it that the child is evaluated by someone qualified to do so. In Pepper's case the behavior was disturbing enough to warrant psychological evaluation even if mental retardation had never been suggested. Unfortunately, many families which live under the circumstances described in Pepper's life do not always receive the medical attention they need. In some cases in which mental deficiency is suspected, medical examination has revealed that the child simply could not see or hear well. In other cases the child may not be retarded but lacking in motivation and initiative due to severe social and cultural deprivation. He may come from a home in which there is no premium placed on education. Many children have been labeled as retarded as a result of their performance on intelligence or achievement tests due to their backgrounds in which communication, both verbal and written, is deficient.

Even children reared in higher socioeconomic levels where great emphasis is placed on books and learning may be regarded as mentally retarded when they may be suffering instead from some personality disorder which is keeping them from functioning at a normal level intellectually.

His intellectual functioning aside, there are several aspects of Pepper's behavior which suggest a need for psychiatric help. These include, among other things, the discord in his immediate family. Most children exposed to so much violence would be expected to suffer emotional trauma. Though we live in a highly mobile society, and some children apparently adjust to moving about with ease, in Pepper's case the frequency with which he moved probably contributed to his difficulties. Most of us need some sense of roots or permanence. For a child it is even more important.

Other causes for concern include his slowness in learning to speak and dress himself, his withdrawal and isolation, lack of curiosity (curiosity being so characteristic of children), and the many problems encountered as a result of the economic, social and cultural stresses in his life.

Whatever the cause, psychological and medical help is important. In most cases such as Pepper's the chances for improvement are greatly increased if treatment is initiated early.

Dean

Dean, a five-year-old boy in kindergarten, had been referred to the mental health clinic by his teacher, Mrs. Adams. The social worker who saw Dean initially learned from Mrs. Adams that Dean had been a disciplinary problem since his first week in kindergarten. Indicating that she had tried to discuss Dean's behavior and attitude with his parents several times, Mrs. Adams had received little cooperation until the parents were told that Dean would have to leave school unless they took steps to prevent his disruption of the class.

Although they were reluctant to do so, Dean's parents made an appointment with Mrs. Jones, the social worker. Expressing considerable anguish, Dean's mother informed Mrs. Jones that Dean had her almost climbing the wall with his frequent temper tantrums and irritability with his brothers and sisters. She had become so upset with his behavior that she had resorted to physical punishment in an attempt to control Dean. For the most part however, even physical threats and frequent spankings had failed to bring about any significant change in Dean's conduct.

Not only did he fight and quarrel with his brothers and sisters for no apparent reason even when they went to great lengths to placate him, his mother revealed that he often fought with other children in the neighborhood. Hardly a week passed but what some irate parent called to complain about Dean's unprovoked attack on his child. That same week he had hit a four-year-old child with a shovel when she accidentally turned over his bucket of sand, injuring her to the point that doctors feared that she might lose the finger almost severed by the blow. At other times he could play with children in the best of humor only to erupt suddenly and violently without cause both verbally and physically.

Physically he complained of headaches and stomachaches often. While highly active at times, both at home and at school, on other occasions he would become very morose and sullen. Obviously a very bright child, his teacher had noticed that he frequently stopped in the middle of a sentence when reading for a few seconds during which he appeared to be somewhat dazed. He would then quickly resume his reading as if nothing had happened. She had seen similar pauses while eating, talking or even playing on the playground.

Indicating that she had to work to help support the family, Dean's mother stated that she was afraid to leave Dean alone for even one minute. One of his brothers or sisters had to be with him at all times when she was away. On two occasions in the past year he had set fires in the house. When they attempted to take him to a movie or shopping with the family, he was into so many things, refusing to mind, to the point that attempts to involve him in family activities had almost ceased. At school his aggressive and impulsive behavior had so alienated his peers that he was seldom invited to participate in the games usually enjoyed by the other children. No matter what he did at work or at play, his tendency to overreact when even the slightest thing went wrong so confused and frightened his playmates as well as their parents that it was usually considered best to avoid Dean whenever possible.

Dean's mother also complained that he often woke up at night afraid and with headaches. On several occasions she had observed that he would suddenly sit up in bed and look around without saying anything as if confused and unaware of what was going on. On another occasion, while dressing for school, he had suddenly stopped, gone upstairs and walked around aimlessly for a few moments, then returned to finish dressing as if nothing had happened.

In the first session with Dean and his parents the social worker was able to learn that Dean had had encephalitis at age two. In the last two years however, he had not been to the doctor on any regular basis for financial reasons. When he did go to the doctor in the agency the doctor was so swamped with patients that he had little time to discuss with Dean and his mother anything more than basic health matters. His behavior at home and at school was never discussed.

From a more comprehensive family history the social worker was able to learn that Dean's two older sisters and two younger brothers were normal with nothing to suggest they had physical or emotional problems. While they fought and argued among themselves and disagreed frequently with peers and parents, there was no evidence they responded so violently or with such unprovoked and intensive aggressiveness as did Dean. While poor, it appeared that Dean's parents provided adequately for the physical needs of their family as well as providing a basically warm and healthy emotional environment.

After several sessions with Dean alone and with the entire family, the social worker recommended that Dean be seen by one of the staff psychiatrists. After one session with the psychiatrist Dean was referred for a more thorough neurological examination. Subsequent neurological findings revealed that Dean suffered from a form of epilepsy. Once diagnosed and medication begun, Dean improved rapidly both at home and in school.

Discussion

Although there are millions of epileptics in this country with some of the most famous people in history having been afflicted with the disorder, the misconceptions and ignorance concerning epilepsy still abound. Perhaps no other disorder is so misunderstood and surrounded by prejudice. Many highly educated and otherwise sophisticated people still refer to victims of epilepsy as being possessed by the devil or evil spirit. It is still common to hear a seizure or convulsion referred to as a fit as if the person were some sort of mad animal to be avoided at all costs. Until recently many states had laws which discriminated unjustly against individuals suffering from epilepsy. Parents have been known to caution their children against playing with some child known to have epilepsy. Most victims have been restricted or suffered social ostracism in some form or other despite the fact that epileptics can function in a normal fashion in most cases.

Most of us know at least one person who has epilepsy. Rare is the teacher who has not been witness to some form of seizure in the classroom in which the child may fall from his seat to the floor with his body jerking spasmodically for a brief period of time. While it is impossible to conceal such an attack, there are literally millions of others who choose to remain anonymous for numerous reasons, who either have seizures of a less obvious nature or else manage to keep them under control with medication. It is estimated that for every case of epilepsy which is diagnosed as such there are probably ten cases in which the proper diagnosis is never made.

This is most unfortunate for in most cases, with proper treatment, seizures can be either completely controlled or frequency of occurrence can be lessened significantly. Henry W. Baird, M.D., in his book, *The Child With Convulsions,* says concerning seizures,

> Overall (if children with febrile convulsions are included), over 90% of individuals with seizures will never have more than one. Over 50% of children with petit mal will not need daily therapy as adults. Over 30% of children with definite idiopathic seizures will eventually be able to do without therapy. Over 90% of children who are otherwise normal can be maintained spell free or with no interference with their daily lives with the use of currently available therapy.[11]

While it is sometimes possible to establish the reason for seizures such as brain damage, tumors, infections or fever, in more cases than not the causes remain unknown even after extensive neurological examination.

In the event of a seizure it is important that parents be notified so that proper medical care can be sought if they are not already aware of the child's condition. While it is obvious to any observer that something is amiss whenever a person loses consciousness and falls to the floor, with the more evident convulsive symptoms being displayed, it should be emphasized that epilepsy can be, and most often is, manifested in less obvious ways. While the following is by no means exhaustive, teachers and parents should be alerted to the possibility of neurological dysfunctioning whenever one or more of the following symptoms are noticed in children:

1. Any loss of consciousness or blackouts if even for brief intervals
2. Falls down with or without jerking movements, head falls forward, arms fly up, etc.
3. Complaints from the child that he has a feeling that something bad is about to happen
4. Complains of funny sensations in parts of body or mentions funny sounds or pictures flashing across his vision, spots before eyes, etc.
5. Any unusual movement, twitching or jerking of any part of the head or body
6. Displays any strange or unusual eye movement
7. Complains of frequent headaches or stomachaches, nausea or vomiting
8. Seems confused or unable to remember events which happened shortly before
9. Frequently becomes very sleepy or falls asleep unexpectedly
10. May not be able to speak coherently
11. Is unduly irritable or easily angered beyond reason
12. Behaves in violent fashion, often fighting or engaging in destructive behavior without cause
13. Cannot remain still or has short attention span
14. Is accident prone, stumbles a lot
15. Behaves strangely after stimulation by music or lights

16. Shows signs of intellectual deterioration or poor judgment often
17. Shows signs of drastic personality changes
18. Evidence of delusions or hallucinations.

Jolene

Jolene, four years old, was brought to the emergency room by her parents, dead on arrival.

Though this was to be her last admission to the emergency room, it was not her first. Her father had on previous occasions brought her to the hospital because of different injuries sustained as the result of accidents. Two and a half years earlier, which marked the beginning of a long series of plausibly explained accidents, Jolene had sustained a severe blow to the head, causing a gash that was bleeding heavily. The father had explained that his daughter had fallen out of her crib.

Subsequently, at approximately two or three-month intervals, Jolene would be brought to the emergency room by her father for various reasons. On one occasion it was explained that Jolene had a broken finger which had gotten caught in a closing door, another time she had slipped and fallen downstairs suffering multiple bruises, then a fractured arm, a torn ear lobe, and so on.

It was always the father who brought Jolene to the emergency room. Bits and pieces of information were drawn out of him which, in sum, revealed that there were five other children at home. The family lived on the brink of poverty. There were frequent quarrels. The mother, by description, was a slovenly housekeeper and left most of the decisions up to the father, who was an unskilled laborer.

The family was intermittently on welfare. Occasionally Jolene was placed in a free nursery by the father but was usually removed by the mother after a week or so. The personnel at the nursery had, on a few occasions, contacted the father to have him carry Jolene to the hospital because of some obvious injury which the parents had chosen to ignore.

Jolene was a quiet, seemingly frightened child. She spoke little. On those instances when taken to the emergency room, she would never respond to questions put to her by members of the hospital staff. When her injuries required admission to the hospital for observation, she did not play with the other children on the pediatric ward. She preferred to remain in her crib.

Despite the history of frequent accidents, she did not appear to be an awkward child. When obliged to ambulate and participate in ward activities, there was no indication that she was poorly coordinated. Nurses' reports disclosed that she was often heard crying to herself during the night. Several times during such admissions her mother had unceremoniously come to the hospital and in an incoherent fashion demanded the release of her child. When the physician in charge would not relent, the mother signed the daughter out against medical advice.

When Jolene was brought in dead to the emergency room, the mother explained in a rambling way that Jolene had locked herself up in the bathroom and would not allow the mother to enter. She further elaborated, saying that there had been a great deal of noise issuing from the bathroom as though Jolene was jumping up and down and banging the appliances. After a while, said the mother, there was silence.

When the father returned home several hours later, she said he broke into the bathroom and found Jolene naked and dead on the floor. Between her legs, was a puddle of coagulated blood that had evidently drained from the child's vagina. The tub water was bloody and leaning against the side of the tub was a broom. The upper end of the handle was splintered and bloody.

The mother further explained that Jolene was a "bad girl" because she was always "playing with herself and putting all kinds of things in her rectum and vagina."

As the mother talked she remained expressionless. The father sobbed uncontrollably.

Because of the circumstances, a coroner's autopsy was performed. The autopsy disclosed evidence of multiple past injuries. Most significant, and the immediate cause of death, was a ruptured liver, perforated intestines and a ruptured uterus. Fragments of wood matching those of the broom handle were found in the abdominal cavity.

A police investigation was instituted. There was no lock on the bathroom door. When interrogating the other children, the police learned little except that the mother was considered to have a bad temper.

At last, the father confessed. He admitted that the mother had been responsible for all of Jolene's injuries in the past. Though he had not been at home, he believed that she probably had killed Jolene.

A psychiatric evaluation of the mother showed her to be psychotic.

Discussion

It is important to note that the events described above occurred in the mid 1960's. The circumstances surrounding Jolene's case may seem revolting if not improbable. Nonetheless these are facts.

Were these events to repeat themselves today it is probable that Jolene would have been identified as a victim of child abuse, otherwise called the *battered child syndrome*. Child abuse has in recent years received considerable publicity through various news and educational media. School teachers, particularly nursery school teachers, are rather well informed regarding the signs of the battered child syndrome. Likewise, emergency room personnel, pediatricians and public health nurses are conversant with the manifestations of child abuse.

By law, any child who is thought to be the *possible* victim of child abuse can be taken into protective custody without legal jeopardy to the accuser. This legal immunity highlights the social recognition that child abuse is not an infrequent phenomenon and further reflects the groundswell of opinion that children, no matter what age, are entitled to medical, psychological and legal protection when there is even the slightest suspicion that the child is the object of parental abuse.

Today Jolene's predicament would, in all likelihood, not have been overlooked. She was statistically within the age range when children are most apt to be abused. Additionally, the frequency of her so-called accidents would have alerted any mildly concerned observer. The egregiousness of her condition could scarcely be missed—broken bones, bruises, her fear and underdeveloped relationship skills shouted for the need for professional intervention.

Because of the wide educational efforts to inform professionals and the public about the cues reflecting child abuse and the relative assurance that the parents involved can profit from treatment, it is probable that the nonabusing parent might well have taken some action to remedy the situation. The starkness and the unmistakable indications of child abuse in Jolene's case can, however, be misleading.

Not all abused children, generally between ages one to five, present so dramatically. There are more subtle manifestations that teachers and parents should be aware of. For example, the babe-in-arms who is chronically malnourished, or bears scratches, or shows signs of being pinched may well be the victim of parental neglect or abuse. Likewise, the two-year-old who exhibits similar signs could well fall in the same category.

There is also the young child who suffers from frequent colds as the result of being kept in an unheated room. Cases of recurring pneumonia may have the same origin. Small children who are left alone to feed and take care of themselves may also be victims of neglect by parents. Bruise marks about the wrist and ankles should raise the suspicion that the child may be tied up while the parents leave the house. A teacher who observes that a child comes to nursery school or kindergarten always tired, sleeping while the other children play or perform their school chores, should question the adequacy of parental care. The child may be prevented from sleeping in a bed. Poorly dressed children from a family that can afford to buy appropriate clothing is another subtle clue that we may be dealing with a more elusive form of child abuse.

The child-abuse entity therefore presents many faces. There may be outright physical damage obvious to all, or at the other end of the abuse spectrum, there may be simply signs of parental negligence that are irreconcilable with the family's economic circumstances and intelligence.

How to approach the parents?

On the surface this may seem a most delicate matter. Experience, however, derived from law officers, teachers, judges, physicians, public health nurses and mental health professionals is consistent in demonstrating that direct confrontation with the parents offers the only hope of getting the parents and child into suitable treatment. Not only do the parents tend to strenuously deny and rationalize the outlandishness of what they often call punishment for misbehavior, they also resist diplomatic tactics to lure them into counseling.

Hence, under the protective auspices of the law, confrontation with the explicit requirement for psychological evaluation is in order. Should the parents not cooperate in a concrete fashion, again the law provides for an alternative in the form of protective custody for the child.

Jolene's parents are not uncharacteristic of the family system that exists when child abuse is at issue. Usually the nonabuser is in collusion with the spouse's aberrations and so is theoretically as guilty and as disturbed by extension as is the victimizing spouse. Women are most often the abusers and usually suffer from severe psychological abnormalities. Men, though less often the culprits, are not infrequently so and are typified by an immature, psychopathic, explosive personality. The parental background of the child abuser has usually been one of violence or neglect on the part of their own parents.

As a final note, though a controversial one—some crib deaths are thought to be at times the consequence of child abuse. On the other hand, researchers are gathering evidence that a congenitally unstable respiratory system that simply quits is the cause of death. Nonetheless, the possibility of child abuse remains.

Rhonda

Rhonda was a small child for her four and a half years. She had long blond hair and was very clean and neat when her parents brought her to the child development clinic. Her mother and stepfather, both in their early twenties, looked young enough to be teenagers and were obviously anxious about what to expect at the clinic.

The parents, Mr. and Mrs. Long, told the social caseworker that they had been married barely a year and were really confused about Rhonda's strange behavior and were seeking help in understanding and managing her. The mother was pregnant and expecting a child within a few months and was also worried about how Rhonda might react to the new sibling in the family. They told the following story about Mrs. Long's first marriage and Rhonda's early life.

Mrs. Long had become pregnant out of wedlock in her senior year of high school. Her mother, with whom she lived alone, was very upset and wanted her to get an abortion or at least give up the child for adoption when it was born. She was also against her daughter's marriage to the high school senior boy whom she considered undesirable and irresponsible. However, Mrs. Long and the boy decided to marry and keep the child. The marriage was stormy almost from the beginning with frequent emotional conflicts between husband and wife.

When Rhonda was eight months old the parents left her with Mrs. Long's mother for one year while they went to live and work in a large city nearby. At the end of that year, Mrs. Long was divorced and returned to live with her mother and daughter.

Mrs. Long was emotionally distraught when she returned home. The strain of her failure in marriage, having an illegitimate child and leaving the child with her mother had left her with great feelings of self-doubt. Moreover, her mother was a strong-willed person and assumed the management and care of Rhonda. Mrs. Long's efforts to assume control of her daughter were usually met with rebuke and ridicule. Mrs. Long found it easier to let her mother exercise control over Rhonda, and eventually found a clerical job in an office. It was there that she met and married her present husband.

Mr. and Mrs. Long were married when Rhonda was about three years old. Over her mother's objections, they took Rhonda to live with them. Rhonda cried and was upset at leaving her grandmother. However, both Mr. and Mrs. Long felt that it would be better for her to live with them.

From the beginning Rhonda seemed afraid to go to bed at night in her room and would cry for an hour or more before going to sleep. After a few nights of this behavior, they decided to let Rhonda sleep with them. Rhonda appeared to enjoy this, but she did not otherwise seem close to her parents. She preferred to play by herself rather than to interact with her parents and did not like to play with any of the other young children in the neighborhood. The parents reported that she would sometimes play with one toy for hours at a time without getting up off the floor or talking to anyone. If they picked her up to hold her, she would resist their attention and express a desire to go elsewhere and play. They took her to visit the grandmother on weekends, but after a few months Rhonda did not seem any happier there than at home.

When Rhonda was four she entered nursery school near her home. Her teachers on several occasions informed Rhonda's parents that she was usually quiet but refused to make any eye contact or talk to the teachers or other students. She frequently stared vacantly around the classroom and sometimes made a humming or singing sound to herself. She refused to play any games or perform most tasks when encouraged to do so. When the teachers gave her a doll or other toy to play with she would usually sit on the floor, quietly holding the doll or toy without speaking or other activity. After a few minutes she would start rocking back and forth slowly, humming to herself. When they tried to pick Rhonda up or hug her she would struggle and whine, never speaking, until the teacher put her down.

Both in nursery school and at home, Rhonda had never had a hearty appetite. If forced to eat something she did not want she would cry and on a few occasions had actually vomited. The parents' concern led them to take Rhonda to a physician. He recommended that Rhonda learn to sleep alone and that she not be forced to eat. Instead he suggested that she be encouraged to eat whenever she was hungry and provided supplementary vitamins.

The parents complied with this advice and were surprised that Rhonda did learn to sleep alone without crying. However, on going into her room one night after she had been in bed for over two hours, they found that she was lying in bed awake. Her diet had become even more restricted. She would by this time eat only four or five different foods.

Still very distraught over Rhonda's behavior, both were hesitant to use force to get her to do anything. Earlier they had tried spanking, cajoling and various kinds of rewards to get her to do what they wanted. By this time, however, the mother, especially, felt so guilty and defeated that she made little effort to correct or direct Rhonda.

The events of the last few weeks had led them to seek professional help at the child development clinic. About two weeks earlier, Mr. Long had been awakened after midnight by a noise in the basement. He went downstairs to find the lights turned on and Rhonda riding her tricycle around in a large circle in the basement. He quietly picked Rhonda up, explained that she should be in bed, and returned her to her room. This same scene was reenacted almost every night for two weeks. Two nights before coming to the clinic, Mr. Long went to the basement to get Rhonda and found several of her dolls and other toys smashed and broken. Neither of the parents slept much that night and early the next day they made an appointment at the child development clinic.

Discussion

Unfortunately, many people are unprepared for the highly important role of parenthood. No diploma or license is required. The lack of preparation for the role of parent is most apparent among teen-age parents. Despite their lack of training for parenthood, however, Mr. and Mrs. Long were alert enough to be concerned about Rhonda's poor appetite, her rejection and fear of social relationships, her overwhelming fear of being alone and her lying awake for hours at night. It was nevertheless very threatening to them to think that they might be the cause of her problems, and it was disheartening to realize that they could not help her change this behavior without professional intervention.

One of the most perplexing realities of childrearing to parents is the difference in reactions of children to similar treatment. One child in a family may thrive on maximum permissiveness or freedom to be self-directing. Yet another child may flounder helplessly unless given frequent direction and control in the growing-up process. The reactions of parents to this kind of uncertainty may vary from anger at the child to extreme guilt feelings over their own perceived inadequacies as parents. It is most important for parents, teachers and mental health workers to understand that children will learn to react in differential fashion in life's situations. A key to helping children grow lies in understanding and accepting these differences. Responding to a child's problems with anger, fear or guilt works against solving the child's problems in a constructive manner.

Another obvious and potential source of difficulty for the young child is inconsistent discipline or warmth of relationships. This is more likely to occur where the parents do not agree on what is best for the child. The child who lives with parents as well as other relatives as did Rhonda or who lives in a series of home environments such as foster homes is often subject to erratic discipline and acceptance. Cooperative action and mutual understanding on the part of adults in these kinds of situations are necessary if the child is to experience the needed consistency of approval. Generally, it is preferable for the parents to exercise control and direction over the child with other members of the extended family working to support the efforts of the parents. It is obvious that such was not always the case in Rhonda's earlier years as evidenced in her difficulty in leaving her grandmother and her attempts to adjust to life with her mother again.

Another warning signal has to do with Rhonda's withdrawal and reluctance to become involved with others outside the home, including her teachers and peers in her nursery class. Children are generally responsive to physical closeness and approval from parents and teachers and desirous of interaction with other children. Although much of the child's play is more toward self than social in orientation until age four or older, it is still important that the child desires interaction with other children. When this desire for closeness and interaction with parents, teachers and peers is missing as was the case with Rhonda, then such should be interpreted that professional help may be needed.

In most cases similar to the one discussed above the parents may also require considerable counseling in order to understand and accept the feelings of alienation that Rhonda had acquired in her brief life. Like many parents, they felt responsible for their child's difficulties with considerable guilt resulting. However, they did take a positive approach in seeking the help of medical and psychological professionals in their efforts to assist Rhonda. It is not always possible to prevent maladaptive behavior, although that is the ideal for which we strive. Where that is not possible, it becomes increasingly important to seek alternative strategies for aiding the child before the maladaptive behavior becomes chronic and debilitating.

Dina

Dina, a seven-year-old child, was seen by the school counselor at the request of Mrs. Collins, her second grade teacher, who had become disturbed by Dina's forgetfulness in class. She also informed the counselor that Dina seemed to be very irritable at times and depressed. Mrs. Collins admitted that she had at first attributed Dina's poor memory to her lack of interest in school and her schoolwork. However, she discovered in talking with Dina's first grade teacher that Dina had been very bright and alert in the first grade with no difficulty in concentration, recall or retention of subject matter.

Concerned about Dina, Mrs. Collins had tried to arrange an appointment with her parents. Before the appointment could be arranged Dina had become ill one afternoon while boarding the school bus for home. Volunteering to drive her home, Mrs. Collins found Dina's father at home still asleep after working the night shift at a nearby industrial plant. Dina's mother had not yet arrived home from her job as a maid in a large downtown motel. The home, a small apartment consisting of four rooms in a housing project, was dirty and sparsely furnished with the rancid odor of garbage thick in the air. It was in these surroundings that Dina lived with her parents and three brothers.

Unaccustomed to visits from teachers, Dina's father, obviously ill at ease, seemed not at all concerned that Dina had been brought home sick. When Mrs. Collins tried to suggest that Dina see a doctor her father said it was unnecessary as Dina had these little upsets often but soon recovered. Although he was reluctant to discuss his daughter further, Mrs. Collins managed to find out that in addition to her frequent spells of nausea Dina also complained of headaches almost daily. Her father also admitted that whereas she had previously been a good natured and happy child, she had become increasingly more difficult to live with in the past few months. Well-coordinated physically for her age, she had enjoyed playing games with her brothers and children in the neighborhood. Recently, however, she had seemed to lose much of her grace and agility. She had stumbled and fallen several times while just walking around the house. Much to her mother's dismay, she had also begun to drop dishes and had turned her milk over on more than one occasion in the past few weeks. Since such items were hard to come by in their household Dina's parents usually responded with criticism or comments about her clumsiness.

Even watching television, one of Dina's favorite pastimes, had become a point of disagreement in the family. Complaining that the picture often seemed out of focus, Dina would try to adjust the set when according to other members of the family there was nothing wrong with the picture. When Dina continued to insist that the picture was blurred, her brothers laughed and told her she needed glasses.

Disturbed even more by what she had heard, Mrs. Collins again talked with Dina's first grade teacher. She was again assured that Dina had been both physically and intellectually alert and seemed to be a very happy and normal child the previous year. Although poor and deprived in many ways, she had approached her school work with enthusiasm and took every opportunity to read any book at her disposal.

As the days passed Dina's irritability and slovenly school work increased. Her moods of despondency and lassitude also seemed to worsen and to occur with greater frequency. She could no longer focus her eyes on the work on the front blackboard. For

the first time she cried in school with complaints of a bad head-
ache. Shortly afterwards she lost consciousness.

She was admitted to the hospital, and after several days of tests
and examinations it was learned that Dina had a brain tumor and
surgery would be necessary.

Discussion

While it is important to be aware of the influence which
psychological forces can have on behavior (verbal, mental, emotional, motoric, etc.), it is also important that we not overlook
the fact that neurological and physiological conditions are capable of masquerading as psychological disturbances. It is most
unfortunate that Dina's parents ignored the serious warning
signals being displayed for so long. Had they acted sooner to seek
medical help, the prognosis would be much more favorable.

Like adults, young children and adolescents have headaches.
Also like adults, the majority of headaches are caused by tension.
However, in children, the sudden onset of headaches dictates a
thorough neurological examination.

Apart from tension a child may experience headaches as a result of a tumorous growth within the brain matter. Such growths
are frequently benign and readily removed with timely surgical
intervention. Other growths may be more serious. Certain tumors,
owing to their slow-growing nature, do not by themselves cause
headaches but may cause eye problems—difficulty in focusing,
dyscoordination of eye movements, double vision, etc. Such eye
aberrations can secondarily cause headaches. The astute general
practitioner is capable of identifying the aberration. Appropriate
referral to an eye doctor or ophthalmologist would clearly be in
order.

As for loss of consciousness, there are many and varied causes,
and such does not always mean that a tumor or some other serious
disorder exists. Within the central nervous system, for example,
there exists a finely balanced neuroendocrine mechanism referred
to as the autonomic system mediated by hormones that cause a
rise or fall in blood pressure. In children and adolescents the
hormonal balance is in a precarious state, especially during

growth spurts and periods of sexual maturation. It is during such developmental surges that syncope (loss of consciousness or passing out) is most likely to occur. Stress, fatigue, skipping breakfast, etc., can cause sufficient insult to an already labile system to the point that the youngster will suddenly lose consciousness because of a drop in blood pressure. Conservative measures such as allowing the child to remain in a reclining position until recovered are usually sufficient. Despite the absence of any serious disorder a physical examination should be stressed, however. Passing out can also be caused by a low-grade form of seizure disorder, tumors, rupture of a brain blood vessel, a blood clot on the brain following a head injury, etc.

Attendant upon physical growth, one often observes clumsiness or poor coordination as the neurological system is in the process of maturing. Nonetheless, a poorly coordinated child who frequently falls or drops things should be seen by a physician. Certain degenerative diseases of the central nervous system tissue may also be the culprit. Congenital hereditary conditions may be manifested through clumsiness also. Not to be ignored as possible causes of neurological problems are such things as malnutrition and exposure to heavy metals (lead, mercury and manganese) as well as infectious viral conditions.

While we have only alluded to a few of the conditions which might cause both mental and physical problems in children, teachers and parents should seek psychological and medical evaluation if the child

1. Suffers a loss of memory regarding recent events
2. Shows signs of mental or intellectual deterioration
3. Has frequent headaches, nausea or vomiting
4. Is clumsy, drops things, falls or stumbles a lot
5. Loses consciousness or has blackout spells
6. Has visual disturbances
7. Shows evidence of drastic changes in personality, i.e. changes from a good-natured person to one who is irritable and grumpy
8. Has convulsions or develops tremors
9. Begins to speak in a slurred fashion or experiences other

difficulties in speaking

/ 10. Seems confused, disoriented, frightened without cause or seems out of touch with reality

11. Sleeps poorly with complaints of terrifying dreams or nightmares often

12. Has bizarre thoughts or behavior

13. Becomes very depressed or lethargic

In conclusion, the importance of medical evaluation should once again be stressed whenever there is reason to suspect that psychological symptoms may be the result of physical disorders. Psychotherapy has never cured a brain tumor, diabetes or a case of lead poisoning.

Missy

Missy, a pretty four-year-old girl, was referred along with her parents to the child guidance clinic by her family physician. Missy's parents had first become concerned about her when she was two years of age. At that time she had become angry with her parents when they refused to let her have a third helping of desert at dinner. Beginning to cry, Missy had become furious when her parents refused to give in to her demands. Commencing to scream even louder, she had lost her breath and fallen to the floor where she appeared to be unconscious with her arms and legs jerking.

In later months the pattern had continued with similar attacks occurring several times each week. At times Missy would cry and then hold her breath for a few seconds after which she would quickly return to normal. On other occasions she would hold her breath until she lost consciousness. Sometimes she would have convulsions. The attacks usually occurred when she was angry at someone or when one of her brothers got more attention than she did.

Afraid that Missy might have epilepsy, her parents had taken her to three different doctors. After examination the results were always the same—no indication of epilepsy. All three doctors had expressed the opinion that Missy would outgrow the attacks;

however the last one had recommended that Missy and her parents seek counseling.

Discussion

Any loss of consciousness or convulsive episode is frightening to parents. There are many things which can cause seizures in children other than epilepsy. These may include metabolic disorders such as hypoglycemia, brain tumors, brain injury, infections, fever and drugs among others.

With Missy's symptoms medical advice should most certainly be obtained. Only a physician is qualified to evaluate and make recommendations in this case.

Fortunately, most children do outgrow breath-holding spells. While it may be difficult at times to distinguish between convulsions of the type experienced by Missy and true epileptic seizures, the causes are quite different.

In those cases in which there may be a conflict between parent and child or some other psychological reason for such behavior, then counseling can be very effective. While it is very probable that Missy's problems were psychological in origin with referral for counseling most appropriate, this type of treatment program should be pursued only after medical evaluation has determined that such is indicated.

Judy

At the suggestion of Judy's kindergarten teacher, her parents brought her to the mental health clinic for help. Judy was a very intelligent and alert little girl, but she did not get along well with other children. She often interrupted the play of other children to tell them they were doing it wrong and then tried to take over and control the other children.

When she was three years old she got mad at a neighbor's puppy that she said was bothering her. She put the little dog in a garbage can and piled rocks on top if it, killing it. She seemed to have no remorse over this incident when her shocked parents questioned her about it.

Judy had one baby sister, age thirteen months. Her mother

said she liked this baby sister although she had occasionally pinched or slapped the baby and made it cry. As a result of this behavior, the mother was afraid to leave Judy alone in the house with the baby. The mother and father once mentioned that it was harmful to a baby to blow in its face. Since that time the mother had twice caught Judy blowing in the baby's face. When her mother questioned her about this, Judy explained that it did not really hurt the baby.

Judy asked questions all the time, according to the parents. She seemed to want to know everything, and when anyone refused to answer her questions she got angry and yelled at them or said they were stupid because they did not know the answer. She expected both parents to stop what they were doing when she wanted attention and usually would not stop bothering them until they did what she wanted.

Once when Judy was at a birthday party down the street, she telephoned her mother telling her that she had cut her foot badly and needed to be taken to a doctor. When the mother arrived, fearful and rushed, Judy explained that she had not been hurt at all but wanted her mother to come quickly to take her home.

Judy was a few months younger than the other children when she entered kindergarten but mastered the academic tasks with ease. By Christmas she could read, write her name and count to a hundred. However, she had no friends in the kindergarten class and said that most of them were stupid. Both her parents and the kindergarten teacher were unsure as to whether she should be encouraged to enter the first grade the next year. Her parents were reasonably successful and aggressive middle-class people who were very upset over Judy's inability to show respect and to get along with others.

Discussion

Many parents-to-be will hope or express openly the desire that their child will be a gifted child. However, not many parents or school systems are ready to cope easily with demands of an intellectually gifted child. The very bright child is apt to be inquisitive, active, aggressive and sometimes intolerant of children who are less gifted.

The gifted child may not be as sensitive to social expectancies as other children because their creative, inquiring minds take them on an exciting exploration of new ideas. Therefore they may not seem to experience the same need for social acceptance as other children. It is not unheard of for the gifted child to fail in school work because he is simply not interested in the routine academic activities required for the majority of children in a classroom. These children may be absorbed in reading great works of literature when the class is dealing with such mundane necessities as dangling participles.

It is nonetheless important for gifted children to learn to make an adequate social adjustment to their environment. Inasmuch as they may become leaders in the community it is perhaps more important that they learn early to get along with others. It is a typical mistake of parents and some schools to push the gifted child into greater and greater academic or intellectual pursuits. On the contrary, gifted children can usually succeed readily in school and have additional time and energy to develop and pursue other interests. For example, the gifted child may readily be able to devote considerable time to music, art, science, drama and various club activities. Developing a wide variety of interests and skills is likely to be more useful to the gifted person than graduating from high school three years early. Just because the child is intellectually gifted does not mean that he or she will excel in social situations or interpersonal relationships.

As was probably the situation where Judy was concerned, the parents of the gifted child sometimes base their love and esteem for the child on the child's intellectual precocity. The rest of the child's faculties and skills are neglected. As a consequence, a sense of personal worthlessness may emerge with attendant feelings of anger and guilt. These feelings may be displayed in the form of displaced hostility or cruelty that serves to allay the anger. The ensuing punishment alleviates the guilt over the anger that is actually felt toward the parents who see their child merely as a valuable commodity rather than a youngster with a variety of developmental needs.

The child who is cruel to other children or household pets is in need of help and understanding. It does not matter whether such a child is gifted or not. The gifted child may need more direction than does a child following a more typical developmental pattern. Therefore it is a mistake for adults to excuse all behavior of a child who is gifted. The gifted child is most in need of flexible and creative adults who sense and are able to contribute to their rapid development.

Tina

Tina was six years old in June and entered the first grade in early September. Her mother brought her to school on the first day and explained to the teacher that Tina was an only child. She expressed some concern that Tina did not seem very interested in other children and was often rude to children who came to visit her. As a result she had no close friends. The mother expressed the hope that school would help Tina become more sociable.

The teacher made a special effort to provide Tina with toys to play with and as other children came in that first day, she took other little girls over to meet Tina. Tina said nothing to the other children, but continued to play with the toys. Suddenly she grabbed a doll away from another girl, hit her hard with it and walked away without saying a word. She walked over to another group of children building a house of blocks and walked through, deliberately kicking the blocks and the partially completed house out of the way. By this time the teacher found it necessary to remove Tina from the other children and talk to her about her conduct when playing with others. Tina seemed to pay little attention to her but said she wanted to go play. When the teacher refused to let her go until she promised not to hit other children, Tina began to scream and fight to get away.

Much of the first day of school was spent with Tina fighting the other children and disrupting what they and the teacher were trying to do. None of the other first graders were yet brave enough to stand up to her so they tried to stay out of her way.

In a conference the next day with the mother the teacher

learned that Tina had twice set fire to some papers and magazines in the basement of their home. The mother had tried both spanking and reasoning with her but with little success. Tina's father, who traveled and was away from home on his job much of the time, said that the only solution to Tina's problem was to whip her hard. He would do this when he was home and Tina seemed afraid of him. She avoided her father and refrained from many of her acts of violence when he was around. However, on the two occasions when she had started the fires in the basement, her father had just left for an out-of-town business trip an hour earlier.

Discussion

One of the most traumatic experiences for the young child is to be unsuccessful in developing adequate social relationships. The basic social skills that develop through parent-child interaction in the first three or four years of life begin to be tried out in child-to-child relationships, usually before entering first grade.

Young children differ, just as do adults, in the manner in which they try to form meaningful relationships. The most successful mode of interpersonal relationships occurs when children are willing both to give and to take. Sometimes the leader, sometimes the follower, it is essential that they learn to cooperate and get along reasonably well with other children. In some unfortunate instances, however, a child feels comfortable only if he or she is the boss or only if playing the role of a follower.

In extreme cases, such as the one illustrated here by Tina, the child learns to be violent, disruptive and almost totally antisocial with other children. These extreme conditions occur infrequently and usually only where the child has very limited contact with others of her age. Obviously, this kind of behavior helps to insure that her contact with peers will be very limited because neither parents nor other children will seek out such relationships.

The parents had not found a suitable approach for changing Tina's behavior and in fact varied so much in their approach to her problem that Tina was more confused than helped by their efforts at discipline.

Once the child enters school or another social group outside the home, such antisocial behavior becomes nonadaptive. It becomes necessary for the child to change such behavior or to leave the school or other social group. In some instances the child may need intensive therapy or counseling before being able to re-enter satisfactorily into the same social group as his agemates.

Patrick

Patrick first came to the child guidance center when he was seven and a half years old. His mother was upset by his uncontrollable behavior both at home and at school. At school he would often run around the room hitting and talking to other children during class lessons. Once he got up on the radiator in the room and ran up and down on it.

His mother reported that Patrick had been on tranquilizers for a year and a half in order to help him gain more self-control. At times he seemed somewhat depressed from the medication but generally was very active, and he engaged in baby-talk or babbling at times. He seemed to have a need to talk and move around all the time.

At home he was frequently mean to his three-year-old sister. He often hit her or took things away from her unless one of their parents was nearby. His mother was pregnant again, and Patrick stated that he hoped this one was not a girl. He also talked frequently about how warm and nice it must be for the baby in his mother's stomach. He sometimes said this to strangers in the home which was very embarrassing to the parents.

Patrick had several boyfriends in the neighborhood that he liked to play with. However, his parents had to restrict his play quite a bit because he sometimes became destructive at another child's home or stayed at another child's home after dark or until his parents went to get him. His mother reported that she usually yelled at Patrick to get him to behave while his father usually resorted to hitting him when he misbehaved. The parents had had several arguments about how to control him.

His table manners were very poor. His spilling and dropping

of food often resulted in unpleasant mealtimes for all. When his parents tried to correct him, his behavior seemed to get worse. They tried having him leave the table and even locked him in a closet, however he did not seem to mind this and on a few occasions had gone into the closet by himself to play.

Despite Patrick's hyperactive behavior, he learned easily and appeared to be quite bright. His teacher said he was one of the most intelligent pupils in class, however his grades were usually poor because he would not always pay attention or complete assignments. He spent considerable time sitting in the principal's office for his misbehavior. His parents had been called to school several times to take him home.

At the suggestion of the family physician, Patrick was checked for possible brain damage. The EEG laboratory reported an unstable brain wave pattern which they considered compatible with mild diffuse brain damage.

Discussion

It is a very agonizing experience for parents to try to cope with a child as hyperactive as Patrick. The possibility that he is suffering from mild brain damage does not make it easier for adults to cope with his erratic and unpredictable behavior. It is understandable that the parents' frustration may often lead them to spank, yell or engage in other behaviors toward the child that contribute to their feelings of guilt as well. Even though many children with Patrick's behavior pattern eventually acquire more self-control as they grow older, the life of the entire family may be disrupted and stressful.

Medication for such lack of self-control may be recommended by a physician, but there is no certainty that this will correct the problem. In addition, the possible disadvantages of large dosages of Ritalin® or other drugs may cause this to be an undesirable option for self-control.

Patience and tolerance by adults responsible for the hyperactive child are very important. However, where there are other children in the family, it may become almost impossible to tolerate this one child's seeming lack of respect for others, thus the hyperactive child is likely to suffer not only from his own disability but from the lack of acceptance from significant adults in his life.

Whenever it is suspected or obvious that a child is hyperactive, medical help should always be obtained. As an adjunct to medical treatment the entire family may profit from counseling as a means of handling their own frustrations and learning to cope with the hyperactive child.

Bill

Bill's parents brought him to the child development learning center. They poured out their concern about his lack of progress in school and alternately blamed the teacher and themselves for his difficulty. Bill was a small, freckled-faced boy who seemed alert to everything going on around him. He smiled easily, responded readily and seemed unconcerned about all his problems. He was barely seven years old and midway through the second semester of first grade.

His first grade teacher had called the parents in early November for a conference. She reported that Bill seemed to be learning slowly and seemed more interested in playing than in concentrating on school tasks. The parents agreed to help and talked to Bill about the need to learn to read, write and know his numbers. Both the parents and his teacher were pleased by Christmas vacation time when Bill could print his first and last name, recognize several letters of the alphabet, and write numerals up to 20. He could count even further than that.

However, when Bill returned to school in early January, he could not write his name or any numerals. He seemed to have forgotten almost all he had learned. After much patient work by the teacher he began to regain some of these skills, but he was falling further behind his classmates. His printing seemed very awkward and shaky and he would often reverse similar letters such as *b* and *d* in reading.

Just prior to the parents' bringing Bill to the child development learning center, his teacher informed the parents that it might be desirable to retain Bill in the first grade for another year. The parents had always thought Bill was as intelligent as their other children. He helped them out in their store and seemed to learn quickly what to do.

They did express a concern for what they called his awkward nature. They explained this by saying he had a lot of accidents such as falling while running or dropping things. One time he had a serious fall from his bicycle which resulted in a severed tendon in his foot. Fortunately it was corrected through surgery.

Discussion

The incidence of specific learning disabilities in children appears to be much more frequent than formerly realized. Many of the children who fail in school seem otherwise intelligent and alert but do not master the reading, writing, arithmetic and related skills of the classroom. Teachers and parents are now becoming more sensitive to the idea that some children develop more slowly than others in their ability to learn through auditory, visual or other methods typically used in schools.

In the case of Bill, intelligence tests that did not involve reading or written words indicated that he had above-average ability. He had not yet developed the ability that other children his age had to learn to read, write and count.

When a child is usually regarded as observant and intelligent at home and in the community but not in school, it is often wise to explore the possibility of a learning disability. Parents and teachers should be alert to the possibility of learning disabilities if the child reverses letters, seems to learn when he hears something but not when he sees it, or vice versa. It is also typical of children with learning disabilities to forget information previously learned or to be unable to concentrate on anything for a long period of time. It is also likely that any child who is unsuccessful in school may soon grow to dislike school and will want to spend more of his time playing or talking to other children.

Many children who have learning disabilities can learn to overcome them if they receive patient and proper training. It may take them two or three years or even longer to begin achieving at the same rate as other children. Obviously, they may also develop emotional problems or feelings of inadequacy because of their inability to do as well as their friends.

Whenever it is observed by parents or teachers that the child is not doing as well in school as outside, help for the child should be sought. A child with such problems will need understanding, praise and support from teachers and parents as he struggles to cope with school work. The child who does not receive this understanding and support from significant people in his life may need counseling in addition to the specialized help or teaching he is receiving.

Marcia

Marcia was the youngest of seven children in a rural family. She entered the first grade when almost seven years old because her mother thought she was a little shy to go to school with other children. She played, laughed and fought with her brothers and sisters but was very dependent on them in many ways. She was slow to make new friends and usually made no effort to speak to someone she did not know. She would stand behind one of her brothers or sisters and wait for them to start a conversation. Her mother and father explained that Marcia had always been a slow starter and had not learned to talk or walk nearly as soon as their other children.

The parents kept Marcia out of school one extra year and then entered her in the first grade. When Marcia sensed that her mother was going to leave her in a strange place with strange people, she clung to her mother's skirt, crying and begging to go home with her. It took a lot of effort by the teacher and mother to get Marcia absorbed in playing with toys long enough for the mother to leave.

Marcia's adjustment to school was slow and very painful for her. On more than one occasion in the first few months her teacher had to get her next older sister in another room to help Marcia stop crying and stay in the classroom.

By the end of November, Marcia was reconciled to staying in her classroom but she did not like to go to school. She would often ask to stay home and had to be encouraged to go to school.

By the end of the school year, Marcia had not learned to read or write except for printing a few letters in her first name. She could count vocally to ten but could not write these numbers. The other children in the class were all more advanced than Marcia, who still spent much of her day playing with toys which the teacher made available. She spent some time coloring although she could not color within the lines on most pictures. She would also ask to have records put on the recordplayer and sit and listen to these for as long as an hour. In other activities her attention could not be held for long. She moved around the classroom quietly but alone. The other children in class would usually leave her alone and accepted Marcia as being different.

Discussion

It seems surprising that parents could live six or seven years with a child and not realize that the child was mentally retarded. This is, of course, more likely to be the case where the parents are uneducated and living in relatively isolated conditions. Under these conditions they do not have as many children outside the home to compare theirs with, nor do they always have the experience or information to make such decisions.

In other cases, although this did not seem to be true with Marcia's parents, the parents deny or refuse to admit that their child is retarded in intellectual development. In such cases the parents may even blame the school for their child's failure to succeed.

Even though Marcia may always be slower to develop, she may learn to function independently in a job and in other social responsibilities; thus it is equally or more important for parents of a retarded child to assist in the child's growth.

A retarded child usually requires more patience and detailed help in learning both social and academic skills. Parents can begin early to read to these children, to help them learn adequate social relationships, and to help them develop the perceptual and motor skills in which they are likely to be deficient. It is especially important for the retarded child to have warmth and acceptance when he begins to realize that he is not like other children.

Whenever it is suspected that a child is mentally retarded, evaluation by someone qualified to do so is essential. There are several indications in Marcia's case which suggest a need for referral for psychological evaluation. These include her shyness; dependence; delay in learning to talk and walk; slowness in learning; alienation and difficulty in meeting people; reluctance to leave her mother; shortness of attention span; strong dislike or fear of school; and lack of ability to color, read or write in comparison to her peers.

While mental retardation should not be equated with mental or nervous disorders, it is sometimes found in people who are mentally ill. As with most families who have a child who is physically or psychologically handicapped in some way, counseling can be very beneficial in helping the other members of the family accept the afflicted person as well as develop realistic expectations in regard to behavior and performance.

Chapter 3

THE MIDDLE GRADES

DURING THE MIDDLE YEARS of childhood, here arbitrarily defined as from eight to thirteen, children are exposed to increasing pressures both from within the home and outside the home. External social pressures become especially great during this period. For most children this is a period when they can no longer have all their needs met by the family group. Parental approval is gradually subordinated to peer approval as they continue the developmental tasks so necessary for the attainment of their own identity and individuality.

Though moving toward independence, children in the middle years are still quite dependent on adults for most of their needs. Their food, clothing, housing and self-esteem must still be furnished, in large part, by adults. They discover, often to their dismay, that there are many adult worlds. They also find that there are many child worlds and often their role in a child world conflicts with their role in the adult world.

Many children appear to adjust and function very effectively during this period and are described as well-adjusted and charming children. Others seem to adapt to change with difficulty. The demands placed on them by the various roles they are expected to assume are too much. Under these circumstances, when children feel seriously threatened or unable to cope with these increasing pressures, they may withdraw entirely, become cruel or abusive, or spend a major portion of their time daydreaming, or they may regress to an earlier infantile stage in which they felt more comfortable and secure. The ways children elect to cope with situations or events which they find intolerable are as numerous as children themselves.

Since children in this age group (as are children of all ages) are so complex and in some ways different from all other children, it is difficult to predict precisely what any one child may do in any given stressful situation. However, the adoption of certain unusual

50

coping mechanisms or ways of relating to one's environment suggest that the child may be experiencing undue emotional distress and subsequently developing ways of responding to life which are unhealthy.

If the child is responding or behaving in a way which is inappropriate or socially unacceptable, then it becomes extremely important during this period for parents and teachers to try to understand the causes underlying the undesirable behavior. To punish children who are not performing in the expected fashion may cause further withdrawal or some other adverse behavior.

While it requires sensitivity and skill on the part of parents and teachers to ferret out the potentially troubled child and assist him in getting the needed help, the price for not doing so is costly for all concerned, especially for the child.

The cases which follow involve children in the age range from eight to thirteen. Most of them are concerned with school-related problems since school is such an integral part of their lives at this age. They include instances in which children are unable to handle the stress in their lives in ways that best facilitate their emotional growth. The efforts of teachers and parents to help in some cases are obvious. In other cases examples are presented in which emotional growth is thwarted by parents and teachers.

The discussion which follows each presentation is designed to stimulate thought and raise questions as to how parents and teachers might be of greater help to children in their quest to adapt to an ever-changing and increasingly complex world.

Marty

Marty, a twelve-year-old sixth grader, came to the community mental health agency after neighbors complained that he had shot their cat with an air rifle.

Conferences with Marty's parents and teachers were arranged when two sessions with Marty produced little in the way of information. Although polite and pleasant, he had volunteered no information about himself and responded to questions with the briefest of answers.

Marty's records revealed that he was of average intelligence, however he had barely passed the last two years. Described by his teachers as a child who had never been a disciplinary problem, all agreed that he was a strange child. By no means shy, he seldom spoke up in class. When he did it was usually in an attempt to be sarcastic or funny. For example, in response to his teacher's request that he give the definition of a monk, Marty had replied with a big laugh that "a monk was a small monkey without a tail."

At other times when he would talk in class he seemed to take great delight in talking of his cruel treatment of animals. Seeming to have developed a penchant for small cats he told of numerous incidents in which he had tried to flush kittens down the commode or had plunged them in a bucket of ice water with a cover so they could not escape. On other occasions he would mix whiskey with their milk or put large amounts of red pepper in their food just to see their reaction. He had received his greatest kick recently when he had watched two cats fight after he had tied them together at opposite ends of a rope and thrown the rope over a tree limb.

Viewed as a loner by his teachers, he seldom played with his schoolmates. Not a good athlete, he was usually seen standing or walking alone at recess in some corner of the schoolyard. When he did seek out companionship it was usually with one of the teachers. One teacher in particular had taken an interest in Marty. As a result he could hardly talk with another teacher or student without Marty coming up and joining in the conversation or more often just hanging around.

Although his fellow students often referred to him as a creep or weirdo, it was usually done in a spirit of fun, and Marty was never subjected to any form of physical punishment. Never seeming to get angry when teased by other boys, he never got in a fight and usually had a smile on his face.

According to his mother his main interest seemed to be television. War pictures in particular were of great interest to him. He liked guns and knives, but since his mother disapproved so strongly of guns he had had to settle for magazines he had collected which dealt primarily with hunting and fishing. Despite his interest in such books he never expressed any interest in hunting or fishing, seemingly satisfied to just look at the pictures.

Discussion

Cruelty to animals in a child Marty's age is disturbing. His mistreatment and torture of animals along with his interest in guns, knives and violence on television is sufficient reason to require further psychological evaluation.

His tendencies to be a loner and his inability to get along with his peers only adds to the picture of a child who might be expected to develop even more serious problems in the future. His ways of getting attention and his relationship with the teacher who showed some interest in him strongly suggest that Marty's ready smile and pleasant disposition are more likely to be his way of covering up the impoverishment he feels in human relationships.

Although it may appear that he is accepting the fun and names poked at him by his classmates in a good-natured fashion, there is reason to suspect that Marty's anger and resentment are coming out in other inappropriate and unhealthy ways.

Not only is it important that Marty be provided with the psychological help he obviously needs for his own sake, it is imperative that he receive help for the safety of others as well. While there is still much to be done before we can come up with a profile of those individuals most apt to commit violence in later years, there are aspects of Marty's background which strongly suggest that he is well on his way toward becoming an explosively violent person.

Kit

Kit, a thirteen-year-old seventh grader, came to see the school counselor stating that he had never had a real friend in his life. He was convinced that even his parents and fifteen-year-old brother were against him. Insisting that his father had always liked his brother better, he had begun to avoid his father whenever possible. This was not hard to do since his father was always at work in his store. He had also learned to dislike and distrust his brother who was always picking on him and saying cruel things to him. He could never have a friend of his own without his brother taking him away.

With his mother, however, it was a different story entirely. Even though Kit was convinced that his mother did not really care for him either, she did spend considerable time with him. Very overprotective, she refused to let him play ball or other sports with boys his age but pushed him into music instead. Carefully choosing all of his friends, she made sure that he associated only with those children who would encourage his interest in music and the "finer things in life."

In discussing his earlier years Kit said that he had done well in school until the fourth grade and had been very happy. For some reason everything began to go wrong in the fourth grade. Even his teachers seemed to pick on him and tried to embarrass him in class. Never very good in sports, both the coaches and students made fun of him on the playground. By this time the thought of going to school had become so depressing to him that he would feign sickness in order to stay at home.

Joining the school band in the sixth grade, he would rush to school in the morning before the other children would arrive and hide in the bandroom until classes began. On the way to class he could still remember how lonely he had been when he saw other students in groups laughing and talking together.

By the end of the sixth grade he said that the constant criticism he received from his father and his teachers had convinced him that there must really be something wrong with him. By the beginning of the seventh grade he stated that he had begun to feel so inferior and so depressed that the thought of getting out of bed in the morning had grown increasingly worse. Whenever he walked on campus he believed that both teachers and students were laughing and talking about him.

Told by his relatives that he never smiled, he admitted that he saw little in life to laugh about. Believing that the best way to get along in the world was to be quiet, he had become more reserved as the months went by. His mother, who referred to him often as a good son and one who would one day make her proud of him, had taken to listening in on his phone conversations. The day before his visit to the school counselor, she had overheard him talking on the phone when he was supposed to be practicing his music and had chastized him severely.

Feeling that he was at the breaking point and so depressed that he had thought of running away from home or killing himself, he had decided to talk with his counselor.

Discussion

Even though he is only thirteen, the degree of distrust and suspicion in Kit's life is alarming. His lack of trust has in all probability played a great part in the many disappointments and failures he has experienced in human relationships. Already well on his way to emotional difficulties unless help is provided shortly, he will in all probability experience even greater psychological misery and distress in the future.

His loneliness and fear of involvement to the point that he would literally hide from human contact only adds to an already dismal prognosis. Whenever fear, distrust and suspicion become so rampant and pervasive as experienced by Kit, such should be viewed as a signal that the child is already experiencing serious emotional problems.

There is also a good chance that Kit will develop problems of sexual identity in the near future unless counseling is begun soon. The domineering, overprotective mother, coupled with the poor relationship with his father, is believed by many authorities to be one of the major causes of homosexual feelings in both males and females.

Kit's seriousness, his absence of a sense of humor, his depression and thoughts of suicide and feigning illness to miss school are additional significant warning signals that serious psychological problems already exist with the need for psychiatric help being imperative.

Lori

Lori, a twelve-year-old fifth grader, was sent to the counselor's office by her teacher who had become worried because Lori looked so sad and depressed. She was also concerned because Lori's grades had been steadily dropping for the past two months. For the first three months of the year she had maintained an A or B average in all her subjects. Since Christmas, however, she had barely made passing grades.

In talking with Ms. Jacobs, the school counselor, Lori agreed that her work had suffered and that she was unhappy much of the time, however she could give no explanation for the change. Things were still pretty much the same in her life. Previously a very enthusiastic and studious person, she stated that she now had little energy and had great difficulty in getting up in the morning. By the middle of the morning she was exhausted. When she tried to study she would become tired and bored easily. She sometimes fell asleep in the middle of an assignment. On both her homework and in class she sometimes left questions incomplete which she had started to answer. Since she had always taken great pride in her work, her poor performance in school had made her feel guilty. At home her sister had made her feel even more guilty when she called her lazy when she felt too tired to complete her chores.

While sitting in the counselor's office Lori complained of nausea and weakness. Concerned by what she saw and heard, Ms. Jacobs obtained Lori's permission to call her mother and urged her to take Lori to a doctor. Three days later Lori returned to inform Ms. Jacobs that the doctor had discovered that she had diabetes. While still not certain, he had also stated that her diabetes was probably causing her depression and lack of energy.

Once treatment began, Lori's condition began to improve and her grades went back up. Continuing to see Ms. Jacobs for several weeks, Lori seemed gradually to accept the fact that she would have to stay on medication for an extended period of time.

Discussion

Endocrine imbalance or body chemistry is believed by many authorities to be the basis for many types of mental disorders. While there is no consensus of opinion regarding the role of chemistry in various mental disturbances, it is known that a number of physical disorders can affect the emotions. Some of these include diabetes, hypoglycemia, thyroid dysfunctioning and anemia among others. The victims may suffer from severe depression, mental retardation, loss of interest and a lack of enthusiasm. In more serious cases they may even become psychotic and have to be hospitalized. In other cases they may suffer from confusion or temporary loss of memory. Some patients suffering from certain physical diseases report they sometimes lose the ability to perform mental tasks once completed with no difficulty.

Some psychiatrists have become so convinced of the importance of the relationship between the physical and the emotional components of human behavior that they insist on a physical examination before they will treat a new patient.

While such may not be essential in most cases, Ms. Jacobs is to be commended for her referral to a physician in Lori's case. Parents and teachers should be aware of the importance of nutrition, drugs and physical health in regard to the mental health of their students and children.

As will be said in several cases throughout this book, the importance of counseling should not be overlooked in dealing with physical illness. Doctors have known for a long time that emotional shock can be just as damaging as physical injury in cases of accident. Unfortunately, we too often ignore the obvious regarding the psychological trauma involved in learning that one has a chronic physical disorder as did Lori. We tend instead to assume once the physical emergency is dealt with, the patient will recover or return to normal functioning. Such is by no means the case. In general it may be stated that most individuals afflicted with such disorders as diabetes, which requires continued treatment, will also suffer some degree of psychological distress. Both parents and teachers should be aware of such and make every effort to see that counseling is available in these cases.

Ana

Ana came to see Ms. Todd, the school psychologist, after she had had sexual intercourse the week before for the first time. Only two weeks away from her fourteenth birthday, Ana indicated that she had met the boy at a drive-in restaurant where she had gone with her girlfriend, Susan, and her boyfriend. After meeting they had agreed to buy some beer and go on a picnic. After drinking several beers one of the boys had suggested they drink some gin which he had stashed in his car. After several drinks Ana stated that she was so drunk that she no longer knew or cared what she was doing. It was at this time that she agreed to have sexual relations with her date. She insisted that she would not have done so if she had not been drinking.

For several days after the loss of her virginity Ana indicated that she had not been upset. She had even dated the person again and had had sex with him although she had not wanted to. They had also gotten drunk again. While driving her home her date had been stopped for drunken driving.

Insisting that she had never been drunk before the previous week, Ana said that she had smoked pot on a number of occasions and used barbiturates as well. While her parents had been upset when they discovered that she had been using drugs, they had agreed that drinking beer was okay.

Saying that she had met a lot of people with considerable ease, Ana was disturbed that none of the relationships seemed to last. Most of her friends were considered emotionally unstable by other students. Several were currently undergoing psychiatric treatment.

Ana had been especially upset in the last few days after the boy she had been dating for two months stopped calling her. Although she had not cared that much for him she had at least felt involved with someone in a relationship which lasted for more than a few days. To prove to her boyfriend that she took the relationship seriously Ana confessed that she had done something that she had never done before. At that point she pulled up her sleeve to show where she had burned her boyfriend's initials in her arm with a cigarette.

When questioned as to why she would do anything which would inflict such pain on her, Ana had replied that the pain had not been that bad. When she had shown the results to her mother her only comment had been, "Why would you do a silly thing like that?" Her mother then proceeded to tell Ana that when she was a small child she would take the scissors and repeatedly stab herself when she became upset.

Shortly before the session was scheduled to be over Ana informed Ms. Todd that she did not want to take up any more of her time as she knew she had other students with more serious problems than hers. When Ms. Todd tried to assure Ana that she was interested in her and her problems, Ana replied, "You really don't care about me. You only listen because it is your job."

Discussion

Ana's need for psychological help is long overdue. Why her parents chose to ignore the earlier warning signals of self-mutilation is a mystery. Such harmful and inappropriate behavior is a signal that something is wrong. Individuals who deliberately inflict punishment on themselves of the sort described in Ana's case have serious emotional problems. Ana's stabbing herself with the scissors and burning herself with cigarettes certainly falls in this category. Equally disturbing is the individual who permits or invites the infliction of pain on herself by others or who inflicts pain on other living creatures.

Ana's rather extensive use of drugs at such an early age is also suggestive of emotional turmoil. While many parents are relieved to discover that their children choose to use alcohol rather than pot or some other drug, there is little cause for complacency. In increasing numbers officials are warning us that more and more young people are becoming addicted to alcohol each year. Of even greater concern is the danger involved whenever alcohol is mixed with other drugs. Such a mixture can be fatal. Even for the older children and adults taking medication prescribed by a physician, the consumption of alcohol with certain medications presents a serious hazard to one's health and should never be indulged in without discussion with the prescribing physician.

Ana's indulgence in such risk-taking behavior (the potentially lethal combination of drugs, driving while drunk, etc.) is still further cause for concern. Her lack of ability to maintain lasting relationships with others is also significant. The low regard she has for herself is demonstrated in her statement to Ms. Todd in which she expresses the opinion that Ms. Todd could not really be interested in her enough to spend even one hour with her. Her attraction to friends who are themselves emotionally unstable may also suggest the need for further evaluation.

Finally, Ana's mother's cavalier attitude regarding her daughter's strange and bizarre behavior raises the question of the emotional stability of the home environment so important at this stage of development for Ana. It is worth noting that unstable families who ignore their own familial problems will tend to isolate a family member like Ana and subtly cause the adolescent to act out their hidden problems. Therefore it is well for the teacher or school counselor to involve the entire family in counseling whenever possible.

Jay

Jay, a thirteen-year old boy, was referred to the school psychologist with the complaint that he could not control his temper. The most recent episode had occurred that morning when Jay pushed a teacher as she had tried to interrupt an argument between Jay and another student.

Though a very handsome boy, Jay had been born with an undeveloped right arm which would never fully develop. Saying that he had at one time been very concerned with his appearance as a result of this physical defect, Jay insisted that he now accepted it and never thought about it anymore.

Jay's parents had been divorced six months earlier with Jay going to live with his mother. However, an older sister had threatened to have Jay taken away from his mother due to the Mother's own emotional instability and drinking problem. Despite her threats to do so, the sister had not followed through because her husband did not want Jay to live with them. Jay said that he did not know where his father was since he had left town after the divorce.

Very courteous and polite in the session, Jay confessed that he had many problems in school with both teachers and students. His sister informed the counselor that Jay had used pity as a smaller child to get attention. When this failed to work as he grew older, he resorted to temper tantrums and threats. At times he would become violent. On several occasions he had turned desks over in school when he became angry, and on one occasion had threatened another student with a knife. His teachers complained that he picked on other students and often fought with smaller children. He had also stolen small sums of money from students' lockers and the teacher's desk on several occasions.

In subsequent sessions Jay began to discuss more freely his physical handicap. Although he had previously maintained that he had learned to live with his physical condition, he now expressed the fear that he would never be able to get a girlfriend or marry and have children. The few dates he had been on had turned out to be unsuccessful in that the girls refused to date him again. He expressed great concern about his sexual development with doubts about his ability to engage in sex. He had become so concerned about the size of his penis, which he believed to be smaller than other boys his size, that he had stopped taking showers in his gym class.

Obviously still bitter about his parents' divorce, Jay said with great intensity, "I would not be in your office today if they had stayed together." While he was unhappy with things as they were with his mother, he asked, "What else can I do? I have no one else to turn to."

Discussion

As with most young children whose parents have divorced, counseling can be helpful. In some cases counseling is essential if the child is to move toward adolescence or adulthood with a minimum of disruption. For most children divorce represents a drastic change in their life-style. The world they have known in many ways no longer exists. Change is inevitable. A great sense of loss, hurt, bewilderment, anger, guilt and concern for the future may exist.

While many of Jay's problems existed prior to the divorce, the breakup of his home probably aggravated the already existing problems. The unstable mother and the environment she provided, along with his sister's threats, only added to his difficulties.

His outbursts, stealing and tendencies toward violence should not be ignored. His life-long physical condition and the resulting doubts about himself physically and sexually are also reasons to recommend that he receive help. Whether male or female, children who express grave concern and doubts about their sexual development should be given attention. Many children will not speak directly to their parents or teachers about such matters as penis or breast size. However such doubts and fears may be reflected in their refusal to take showers in the presence of their classmates, wear a swimsuit or go out on dates.

Sometimes such fears can be allayed by a sensitive teacher or parents by correcting many of the sexual misconceptions which have originated due to a lack of adequate sex education, both at home and at school. In those cases where there is some organic basis for sexual concerns or embarrassment to the child such as an undescended testicle, menstrual difficulties or lack of physical development, evaluation by a physician is most important. Since Jay already had one birth defect, a medical evaluation should be recommended. Not uncommonly, when one birth defect exists, the likelihood of others is increased. Additionally, and in the same vein, though his temper outbursts were probably psychological in origin, the possibility of a defect of the brain tissue associated with seizure-like outbursts should not be overlooked.

Manuel

Manuel was three when his father left him and his mother to fend for themselves. Both his parents were foreign-born and had come to this country in hope of a better life. The father was unskilled, and this fact together with his lack of any specialized work skill made it difficult for him to find or keep a job. Eventually the frustration of a different culture and repeated failures led the parents to much quarrelling and excessive use of alcohol by the father. After one violent argument between the parents in which Manuel's mother was beaten and accused by the father of going out with other men, the father deserted his family.

Manuel remembered his father only vaguely by the time he was ten. By then his own life had been filled with so many experiences that his father remained as a dim but happy figure who laughed easily and pitched him into the air.

Manuel had known what it was to be hungry for almost as long as he could remember. He also knew there were many ways to get money from people if you were clever. One way was to take money when the owners were not looking, but he had discovered that you were likely to get caught at this. He also knew the results of being caught were very unpleasant. His favorite way to get money was from the college students in the city where he lived. He found them an easy touch for begging or occasionally he would run an errand for them for a dime or a quarter.

His mother was away from home so much that Manuel began to seek the companionship of college students or anyone else he could find. Even when his mother came home it was usually with a different man and they usually never wanted Manuel around. Sometimes the man with his mother would give him enough money to go to a movie for the evening. By the time Manuel was seven he had learned many ways to con people out of money.

Manuel was approached by three college boys one day and asked if he would like to make a lot of money. He agreed but, street-wise, insisted on having the money first. They paid him five dollars to perform homosexual acts with the three of them. Manuel thought this was a strange but easy way to make money. The college boys also told him what a good boy he was and he did like to get the praise. For two years, this was Manuel's main way to get money when he needed it. He could get five dollars every week or two this way and he almost gave up trying to swipe it from kids at school or begging for it. He was upset when he found these boys were graduating and leaving the college. He began to ask other boys in the college dorm if they would like to pay him to perform similar acts for them. This behavior resulted in Manuel being referred to juvenile authorities.

Discussion

Young children may get involved in sexual activities in a variety of ways. Some sexual activities by children, even those of pre-school age, are quite normal and exploratory activities. A child is usually interested in his own body and its function, and young children may be puzzled and interested in the different anatomy of a child of the opposite sex.

There is also warmth and assurance that results from one human body in close contact with another. Therefore, it is not unusual to find boys, even into teenage years, walking happily down the street with their arms around each other. Among girls this close physical relationship may be tolerated until an older age, but boys begin to encounter an early social resistance toward physical contact with other boys.

In other instances the child's first sexual experiences may be of an exploitative nature. The young girl may be raped or coerced into engaging in illicit sexual relationships. Sometimes the girl's first sexual experiences may even be incestuous, forced upon her by a father, older brother or other member of the family. In like manner, young boys may agree to homosexual relationships—very infrequently to heterosexual relationships—for praise and attention, for money or because they are threatened or forced into such relationships.

Sexual relationships are the most intimate of all personal relationships and, if accompanied by violence, may result in serious emotional problems for the child. In like manner, if sexual relations are perceived by the young child as merely a way to manipulate people or to get what you want, then there is often difficulty in the child forming meaningful interpersonal relationships. In Manuel's case he was perceived by adult juvenile court workers as a "bright, pleasant little con-man." He had had little opportunity to form positive, trusting relationships with anyone. Stealing, begging and homosexual acts for Manuel were only the techniques necessary to eat and to survive.

Addie

Addie, a twelve-year old girl, well-developed physically for her age, was referred to the mental health agency by her pastor, Reverend Harris, as the result of a session between Addie's mother and Reverend Harris the week before. In making the referral, Reverend Harris had informed the social worker that Addie's mother had found Addie and her father in bed together one night after he thought his wife had retired for the evening. The father, a very wealthy and prominent professional person in the community had been nude. Addie was clad only in her pajama top.

At first threatening to divorce her husband, Addie's mother had relented and agreed to give him another chance. However, she had remained so upset that she finally arranged the appointment with Reverend Harris without her husband's knowledge.

During the session with Addie it was learned that the sexual relationship with her father had been going on for over two years. Though she insisted that she did not like it, she stated that she had been afraid to resist her father's advances. While considering telling her mother, she had never done so. She had told her older sister who had advised her not to mention it to her mother, informing Addie that her father had also made similar advances toward her but stopped when she became angry.

In discussing the relationship Addie described the scene as one in which her father would come to her bedroom at least once each week, usually after his wife had retired for the night and he had remained up to read or watch a late television program. She could usually hear him coming up the stairs and would often feign sleep with the hope that he would go away. This usually did not deter him, however, as he would climb into bed with her anyway. As described by Addie he would then begin to run his hands over her body or lie beside her with his penis rubbing against her. In response to the question regarding sexual intercourse, Addie insisted that she could not remember if actual intercourse had occurred or not. She did say that she had wondered why her mother had not become suspicious long before about her husband's weekly visits to her room and had not done something about the situation.

After two more sessions with the social worker Addie was referred for sessions with a psychiatrist.

Discussion

Sexual relationships between siblings, and especially between parent and child, are taboo in almost every culture or subculture in the world. Incest between parent and child is not only an indication of serious problems in the area of psychosexual development for the two people involved, but usually indicates that something is seriously wrong in the entire family structure. At best it has a devastating effect on other members of the family. Not only does socially prohibited sexual intimacy take place between parent (usually the father) and child, but also both parents fail in one fashion or other to provide adequate role models.

Incest may occur between father and son as well as between father and daughter. It occurs with much less frequency between mother and child. While we often think of incest as occurring in lower class groups of people, it can, and does, happen at all socio-economic levels. While we see an occasional article in which parents are encouraged to teach their children how to masturbate or even encourage siblings to have intercourse with each other as if such were just another form of family recreation, we cannot agree that such training will be emotionally healthy.

Experience in counseling with older adolescents and young adults has indicated that children who have been reared in a home where they were the victims of incestuous relationships generally suffer severe problems of adjustment, both now and in later life, sexually and otherwise.

A word of caution—It should be emphasized that we distinguish between incest and the normal curiosity a child displays about the sexual organs of both parents and siblings. It is not unusual for a small child to try to fondle the father's penis or the mother's breasts. Siblings quite often experiment with each other sexually. If this continues into later life, however, it is a different matter. Certainly any parent who encourages sexual contact between parent and child is in need of psychological help.

The excessive and premature exposure of a child to sexual activity with a sibling or parent tends to arouse passions that cannot be appropriately channeled into age-appropriate behavior such as in early adolescents' excursion into the realm of tentative sexual play with peers of the same sex, usually followed by trials of heterosexual behavior. In the case of incest the child's sexual aims become closely bound to the culpable parent. Though ridden with crippling guilt, the child often feels special and superior, and thus ceases to mature sexually in a normal way. Additionally, the guilt must be expiated. Retribution usually takes the form of different acts of self-destructive behavior.

Eric

Eric was the smallest boy in his fourth grade class and seemed always to be moving about the room. He was new to the school system that year and the other children had been slow to accept him as a member of any group. He was teased by several of the boys for his small size. However, he never seemed to get angry at them or fight back. A few of the girls began to talk to him first, and later some of the boys also. He was really hard to resist for long because he spent a lot of time talking to the other children and never tried to dominate them and was never aggressive toward them. He would accept a place on the worst ball team readily or be last in line for lunch or playground and never complain.

He soon became much more popular with the children than with his teacher. Mrs. Wright was known to be a flexible and understanding teacher who could tolerate quite a bit of noise and activity from children, but Eric had become too much even for her. Anytime she gave the children an in-seat assignment, Eric would find an excuse to talk to another child or to her about it. Even though she reminded him frequently to stay in his seat and rewarded him with much praise when he did, she found him disrupting other pupils in the classroom daily.

Eric was also disturbing to Mrs. Wright because he came to the present school system and her classroom with better-than-average grades. In her classroom he was barely passing in any academic area and seemed not to be improving. His ability level was listed on school records as above average and his father taught at the local college. Everything seemed to indicate that Eric should be a superior student, and Mrs. Wright began to feel a bit guilty that she was not able to help Eric achieve more.

She decided to talk to Eric about his inattentiveness once more and inform him that she would have to call in his parents for a conference if his behavior did not change. Eric, with seriousness and eagerness, promised that he would work on his behavior. He then spent the rest of the day talking to other children in the classroom every chance he got. Some of the other pupils were also beginning to regard him as a nuisance by this time.

Mrs. Wright called Eric's mother, who agreed to come to

school the next day. She indicated that her husband could not come with her. Eric's mother seemed to be genuinely interested in Eric and agreed to talk to him about his behavior in school and to help him with homework. She seemed tense and distraught throughout much of the interview. When the teacher asked her if her husband would also help with Eric, she started crying. Eric's mother then explained that her husband had left home two months ago and that there were impending plans for a divorce. She explained that she and her husband had experienced serious marital conflicts for the last eighteen months. Much of the conflict had centered around childrearing with the mother wanting more parental structure and direction for the children than her husband. She indicated that Eric seemed especially upset over their marital differences, perhaps because he was the oldest child and also because he had been very close to his father. She felt very anxious because she did not know how to fill this void in Eric's life, yet also felt certain that she and her husband would not be reconciled.

Discussion

There are many children who are labeled as hyperactive, yet not too many of them are considered very unusual outside of a school setting. When they are not in a highly structured learning situation they may appear to be reasonably normal, active children. Nevertheless, there are some children who really seem driven to action which neither the present circumstances nor their past history seems to warrant. Such children may be undergoing a very stressful emotional experience with which they are unable to cope. It may be a temporary crisis or it can be the beginning of a continuing conflict which the child cannot resolve. If so, the unresolved conflict will continue to sap his strength and limit his effectiveness.

The teacher in Eric's case was at somewhat of a disadvantage in this instance because she did not know Eric's previous behavioral history. She could, as she did, infer that his previous good academic ability and achievement probably meant that he had not always exhibited this behavior.

Generally, children who make a great effort toward social interaction with other pupils at the expense of teacher criticism are experiencing some kind of conflict. One typical kind of conflict occurs when the child feels so inadequate at academic achievement that he can get no reward through that kind of activity. Then he often seeks to get the reinforcement that every child needs through the approval of his peers. Another common cause of seeking undue approval from peers occurs when the child is under unusual stress at home or at school. He may feel singled out by the teacher as undesirable. He or she may also feel so rejected at home that unusual peer support is sought. This latter explanation was more the case for Eric who simply could not deal with the conflict between the two parents whom he loved.

Some of the signs that a teacher, school psychologist, counselor or parent can be alert to are:

1. Any sudden change in the child's level of activity. Either a considerable increase or decrease in this level may be significant.

2. A decreased level of school achievement from year to year or month to month may be significant. There may be a rational explanation for this change such as a more difficult curriculum. In any case, the change is cause for some evaluation of the situation by the concerned educator.

3. An unusual need for peer attention or approval suggests the child is not getting approval elsewhere.

It is a wise educational policy to have an early contact with parents of all children new to a community or school. It is also advisable to schedule an early meeting with parents any time a child seems to have a problem in school.

Arnie

Arnie, a twelve-year-old fifth grade boy, was new to the school this year. He was a thin, handsome boy who rarely ever looked anyone in the eye. His teacher and most of the other pupils took this as an indication of his shyness at being new in the neighborhood.

Soon after Arnie entered the class, pupils began reporting that pens, coins or other personal belongings were missing. Arnie reported one day that he too had had a quarter in his desk that was now missing. Neither the pupils nor teacher could find the thief.

One day the teacher noticed Arnie missing from the playground and returned to the classroom to find him looking through desks and putting things into his pocket. He denied that he was taking anything but said he was looking for his lost quarter. His teacher forced him to empty his pockets which contained some coins and several pens. The returning pupils identified pens that he had taken, including some that were marked.

Arnie had a long history of stealing, apparently starting years before with his mother's purse at home. When he found that she objected only slightly or even failed to notice his petty thievery, he decided to try his skill in stores and elsewhere. Successful in his earliest attempts, he was eventually caught at ten years of age taking several packages of candy from a store. Because of his age his parents were called in, and Ernie was warned not to repeat this behavior.

Six months later he was again caught trying to take a small camera from a store. Despite severe punishment by his parents for this offense and a stern warning from juvenile court officials, Arnie persisted in his thefts. In a belief that a change of surroundings would help, his parents moved to a new community hoping that Arnie would meet new friends and escape his reputation as a liar and thief.

When the teacher in the new school contacted his parents about Arnie's behavior, the parents were distraught and asked the teacher how they could get help for Arnie. They were finally convinced that the source of his problem must be emotional since he had no real need for the things he stole.

Discussion

It is not unusual for children to steal a few minor things as they are growing up. In fact, many youngsters are allowed by their parents to take money without asking when they want to get an occasional coke or ice cream. It is also quite common for children to find objects on the playground or on the street and not bother to return or report the lost article. However, these instances, while somewhat related to Arnie's problem, are regarded as normal. In the case of Arnie and other similar children, stealing and the accompanying lie when confronted become an almost uncontrollable urge. Such children will steal almost anything with little regard for whether they need it or not. They may even accumulate a collection of stolen articles that they will look at and add to periodically.

Obviously, when the problem reaches the severity of Arnie's, then there is need for a full exploration of the child's emotional needs. In some cases he may feel neglected or rejected by his parents. In other instances, the child may have a strong need for success or to improve his feelings of self-worth, and will unfortunately hit on the notion of collecting stolen articles. For many children also, the thrill and excitement of stealing something without being caught is a stimulating factor. Children may lie to cover an obvious guilt but also as a way of flouting authority and proving to themselves that they are more clever than a feared authority figure.

It is also often the case that the persistent liar and thief has a deep fear or distrust of other people. He or she, as was typical of Arnie, may really be afraid to face up to people, eye-to-eye, and instead seek devious ways of getting attention and proving a kind of superiority over others.

Children who steal and lie repeatedly, particularly when they steal objects not really needed or useful to them, are asking for psychological help. Parents and school officials who are sensitive to these needs will seek professional help for the child.

Walter

Walter was nine years old when he first came to the attention of the school counselor. His teacher reported that although he had been a good student with good grades two years earlier, he was now failing in all subjects. Moreover, Walter was restless and inattentive in class. On two recent occasions, he left the classroom, supposedly to go to the bathroom, but he left the school instead. He seemed preoccupied much of the time with his own concerns rather than school work. His mother complained that she had had difficulty in getting him to go to school for the last year. Some mornings he would become so ill when she woke him up for school that he would throw up. Despite his crying and protesting, however, she made him go even if she had to drive him to school herself.

Walter's mother had remarried when he was four years old and now had three children. Walter was the oldest. Her second husband had left her over a year ago. Since that time she had lived with a variety of different men in the home. Walter was often left in charge of the younger children while his mother entertained men both in and away from her home. Having grown very fond of his step-father, who had often taken him hunting, fishing or for a hike in the woods, Walter strongly resented the men who had taken his step-father's place in his mother's life.

Walter frequently mentioned to his teacher that his Daddy was going to come for him that weekend and take him to live with him. Once when he ran away from school he said that he was going to meet his Daddy. He became more reluctant to go home at all and frequently would stay away until it was dark. His mother would occasionally beat him for this behavior but usually failed to notice that he was gone unless she needed him to care for the other children.

After several absences from home and school, his mother reported him to juvenile authorities as being incorrigible. Juvenile authorities then contacted the school to seek the assistance of the school counselor.

Discussion

Sometimes the socially unacceptable behavior of children seems to be based on a wise choice under the given circumstances. Although the rules of our society require children of a certain age to attend school and to live at home, there are a few circumstances when either of those options can be very undesirable. Certainly the school had done nothing intentionally to compound Walter's problem, but the demands of learning and concentrating on academic tasks were simply too much for him at that time. His shock and hurt over losing the only adult support that he had at home was too great for him to concentrate or achieve in school.

Occasionally a home situation can be more damaging psychologically and emotionally to a child than any other influence in his life. When this is the case, the major source for emotional support for the child is gone. Despite the efforts of schools and other social institutions, it is still the home situation that should give the most direction and support for the child's emotional growth.

Many young children, when confronted with such a dramatic withdrawal of meaningful adult relationships, will seek escape as the only way of coping with this trauma. At a younger age they may develop imaginary friends to replace the parent that is lost, or they may simply and literally try to run away from the bad situation to a place where they think things will be better. Some develop school phobias.

For reasons similar to this many young children who need some semblance of acceptance may allow themselves to fall under the influence of older and sometimes devious children or adults. To the child who feels alone and without support, the promise of friendship and lasting companionship can cause him, out of loyalty to the gang, to commit many acts considered socially unacceptable. Though the acts are sometimes reprehensible, behavioral change will take place only if the noxious motivating influences are eliminated.

Rather than punishment, children like Walter need help. Counseling is definitely recommended.

Trudy

Trudy was a very attractive and mature young girl for her twelve and a half years. She was brought to the mental health clinic by her married sister with whom she lived. Both of Trudy's parents were killed in an automobile accident when she was eight, and she had gone to live with her older sister who had married just before the accident. A year later Trudy had gone to live with her grandmother, in her seventies. However, Trudy's sister reported that her grandmother was too old to watch over Trudy.

Trudy had started her menstrual cycle about the time she went to live with her grandmother. This physical change and her grandmother's lack of supervision had caused Trudy to become boy crazy according to the sister. The sister took Trudy back home to live with her when the grandmother reported she was staying out all night with some older boys in the neighborhood.

Trudy was the center of numerous family arguments in the sister's home. Her husband really did not like Trudy very much and felt she was a bad influence on their own two small children. As a result, he objected to Trudy living with them and thought she should be sent to a foster home since there were no other relatives for her to live with. The sister did not want her in her home either but felt a responsibility for her only sister.

Trudy seemed to be jealous of the attention the parents paid their own children, and she would pout and cry if she felt slighted in this regard. Even though her sister punished her and told her not to go out with any boys at her age, Trudy would sometimes slip away from home or school with older boys. She was out one night with some boys until 4:00 A.M. and her sister had telephoned the police to look for her.

Trudy was never an excellent student, but in the last two years she had barely managed to pass from one grade to the next. She complained of headaches and other illnesses in order to miss school and said that her teachers did not like her.

Despite punishment and pleading on the part of the sister and her husband, Trudy would not obey them and continued to run off with a variety of boys. Her sister had contacted the family physician to put Trudy on the pill to protect her from possible pregnancy.

Discussion

It is certainly a traumatic experience for any child to lose a parent by death. When the child loses both parents and has no similarly-aged siblings or caring adults to rely on, the emotional scars go even deeper. It is all too often the case that such orphaned children are thrust upon a relative who is emotionally or even physically unable to assume the responsibility for the child's needs. The child, thus orphaned, may arouse feelings of both guilt and rejection in the relative who is trying to take the place of deceased parents.

The number of children living in the homes of relatives or in foster homes is larger than might be expected. Most typically the relative who plays the guardian role is a grandmother, often ill-equipped emotionally, physically and financially to care for a young child. Perhaps cast suddenly from the role of a doting grandparent to that of disciplinarian, the direction given may be weak and vacillating. The accompanying failures and indecision of the child contributes to the difficulty of such an adjustment.

In those instances where the child is forced to live with an older brother or sister who is married, it is difficult for the orphaned child to be accepted as a member of the family. An otherwise slightly unstable family may be torn apart by the conflict over this intrusion into their life. The sister or brother may be blamed by their spouse for bringing this disruption into the home.

It is understandable that a young child such as Trudy may desperately need and seek love and acceptance on her own. In Trudy's case, a young and very attractive girl, she found it easy to obtain admiration and company of boys. From Trudy's perspective the risk of social rejection and disapproval by her guardians was minor compared to her need for approval by her peers. In Trudy's case, distorted parental gratification is being sought through sexual acting out with her peers. Age-appropriate peer interaction is in large measure determined by the acquisition, from a *good* parental figure, of a set of values that will govern peer interaction which is becoming to the child in elementary school. Trudy needs first and foremost a stable, loving, consistent parental figure who approves of Trudy as a needy youngster. If such is provided, good peer relationships will probably follow automatically.

Anne

Anne was regarded as being the most unpopular girl in her fourth grade class. Without success, her teacher had tried to prevent the other pupils from teasing Anne, who was fifty pounds overweight. Though Anne was energetic, she was never really able to run nor play games with the other girls because of her weight. As a result, she was always chosen last for any team games, with resulting giggles and comments about her inability to perform.

She always seemed to be perspiring, and other children commented about her unpleasant body odor. She did not fit comfortably into the classroom desks nor participate in the noisy banter of fourth grade pupils.

Both of Anne's parents were overweight so she had not had much, if any, criticism about her weight prior to entering school. Her parents often rewarded her with candy or other sweets for good behavior. They would often comment on what a good eater she was and bragged about how she could eat more of some foods than anyone.

It was almost impossible for her mother to find any clothes in the local stores to fit her so she made most of Anne's clothes. Regardless of how well her mother tried to design and make her clothes, Anne never seemed to look as neat and clean as the other children.

Anne had learned to expect and take some of the criticism she received from other children. In a feeble effort to belong she would sometimes laugh at herself along with the other children when they made comments about her weight problem. However, it was obvious that she was lonely and felt rejected by others. She was usually by herself in the hallways or playground and several times had been noticed talking to herself.

Her teacher had tried tactfully to suggest that she might want to lose some weight. Even though Anne agreed with this idea, she seemed unable to control her eating habits and was always nibbling on a candy bar or other food.

Discussion

It is not unusual for the growing child to be moderately overweight at some period of childhood. Emotional stresses, the amount of physical activity the child engages in, and family eating habits are all factors in the child's gaining or losing weight. However, when the child has been grossly overweight since birth, as was the case with Anne, then it is obvious that the child has both a physical and a mental health problem. Excess weight tends to be viewed in a very negative way in our society so that the overweight child is almost certain to be criticized and ridiculed by other children. Excess weight is also generally regarded by physicians as a contributing factor to certain physical health problems such as delayed onset of menstruation and, in later years, diabetes and high blood pressure.

The child is usually influenced greatly by the attitudes of parents. If the parents eat excessively, there is a greater likelihood that the children will also. Perhaps too frequently parents will resort to providing the child with ice cream or candy as a reward for good behavior or to soothe an injured knee. Thus, the child may learn to associate eating with pleasant feelings. In extreme cases the child hardly feels comfortable unless he is eating or drinking.

It is also natural for the concerned parent to want his child to grow in physical stature as well as in other ways. It is quite common for parents to show some pride that the child is eating, growing healthy and big. When the parents themselves are overweight there may be subtle pressure on the child to look and act like other members of the family.

It is now generally understood by most people that mental health and physical health are related. The person who has a physical disease or sickness is not likely to be at his best emotionally. In like manner, continuing emotional stress and upset can sap the child's physical stamina. If we are to enhance the child's chances for success in school and society, it is important to help him develop the best possible physical and mental health habits.

In most cases in which children are noticeably overweight the causes are psychological rather than physiological. If the overweight child does not already have psychological problems, the criticism and rejection he is apt to encounter will probably contribute to considerable emotional stress. Since drastic weight problems can be both cause and effect in regard to emotional distress, counseling can be helpful and is encouraged.

Steve

Steve was larger than any other children in the class, and he never failed to remind the other boys of this fact. Although he was rather subdued and obedient in class, he was viewed with fear or dislike by many of the other boys in his class.

In the hallways and the playground, when no teachers were nearby, he delighted in beating up and shoving around many of the other boys. Most of the boys avoided him and ran away when he came near. However, a few of the boys looked upon him with admiration and readily became his followers.

Steve was now in the sixth grade and twelve years old. His school work had never been good. He would always do barely enough to pass. He openly boasted to the other children that school was sissy stuff and that he planned to quit as soon as he was sixteen. The other children knew that he sometimes smoked cigarettes and also that he skipped school at least once or twice a month.

The sixth grade teacher was teaching for her first year, and in her eagerness to be fair and open with all students, was quite permissive. Steve soon sensed this and began to cause increasing disorder in the classroom. When he realized that the new teacher was slow to enforce rules, he talked out during study time and hit and pinched the other pupils. When the teacher tried to reprimand him for his behavior, he blurted out boldly that his dad said all teachers were lazy and stupid and that because he paid their salary with his taxes, they had no right to tell his son what to do.

Discussion

It is fairly typical for growing boys to want to test their physical strength, particularly in games and contests with other children near their own age. However, this is a quite different need than the one expressed by the bully who wants to hit and hurt people as a general way of life.

Beneath Steve's obedience to authority figures that he feared or respected lay feelings of hostility that he would express and vent upon anyone whom he did not fear. In fact, such children often delight in the discomfort and pain of others.

Steve indicated in his intense desire to be supermasculine some fears that he might not be as he wanted. He also revealed that his father had some of the same contempt and hostility toward authority figures that he expressed. Although children need parental support when things go wrong, the father's siding with Steve against his teachers is unfortunate.

Steve's rebelliousness and extreme need to be tough may be of little value to him once he gets out of school and desires to enter the job market. Even though some employees may desire the physically strong applicant, few are seeking a potential troublemaker. The class bully is often the child most in need of counseling, psychological services or other professional help for healthy emotional development.

Molly

Molly, a pretty eleven-year-old child in the fifth grade, was brought to the child guidance clinic after her grandmother had surprised her masturbating in the bathroom. After scolding Molly the grandmother had a heart-to-heart talk with Molly's mother and convinced her that Molly needed help with her *problem*.

In the first session with the counselor, Ms. Horne, Molly's mother revealed that she had caught Molly playing with herself on two other occasions over the past two years. The first time she had screamed and yelled until Molly had retreated in shame to her bedroom. On the second occasion she had found Molly standing nude before her mirror fondling her small breasts one night after she had gone to Molly's room to ask her to turn her stereo down. Thinking that another approach might succeed where the first one had failed, Molly's mother decided to talk and reason with Molly in a more mature fashion about the serious effects masturbation could have on children, not only now but in the future.

In the second session alone with Ms. Horne, Molly admitted that she knew it was both sinful and harmful to masturbate. Despite her convictions she confessed that she had continued to do so on occasion. After each episode, overwhelmed with guilt, she would vow never to masturbate again if God would only forgive her. However her promises were eventually ignored when after some time she would again indulge in playing with herself. Each time, convinced that she was not only doing something physically harmful to herself, the broken promises only added to her guilt and feelings that she was engaging in behavior which was shameful and sinful.

After several sessions with Molly's mother, Ms. Horne managed to convey that masturbation was not in itself a sign of emotional problems or mental illness in children and adolescents. With the mother's permission Molly continued to be seen for individual sessions with Molly gradually learning to view sexual feelings and needs as a normal part of growing up.

Discussion

Most children masturbate or engage in other forms of sexual experimentation alone or with other children. Despite the myths to the contrary there is no scientific evidence that masturbation in children or adolescents is harmful physically. It can result in emotional damage if the child is made to feel guilty or abnormal because he masturbates. Otherwise, there is no evidence that masturbation is emotionally harmful either.

Sexual desires and curiosity are normal among children of all ages. Even small babies soon discover their sexual organs and the pleasurable sensations which can be experienced while fondling the genitals. Rather than dangerous or harmful, sexual curiosity and experimentation are desirable if the child is developing both physically and emotionally. Masturbation does not cause brain damage, wrinkles, dark circles under the eyes, damage to the sex organs or the myriad other symptoms attributed to autoeroticism. Neither does it cause impotence or frigidity or other sexual dysfunctioning in adulthood unless again the person has been made to feel that something is seriously wrong as a consequence of his masturbation.

On the contrary, a number of older adolescents and adults who come for counseling with sexual problems say they have never masturbated. While the absence of masturbation is probably not the cause of their sexual difficulties in later life, it does suggest that these individuals have perhaps been reared in a severely restrictive and rigid environment in which any expression or thoughts of sexual feelings were anathema. Such rigid thinking is more often the culprit where sexual problems are concerned than is the matter of masturbating or not masturbating.

In summary it might be said that masturbation or the absence of masturbation in itself neither causes or prevents sexual problems. The absence of sexual curiosity or masturbation may mean, however, that the sexual climate is one in which normal sexual desires and expression are neither encouraged nor permitted. On the other hand, masturbation in children of both sexes, without guilt or embarrassment, can mean that children are developing a healthy and accepting attitude toward themselves sexually.

The wise parent does not scream, chastise or embarrass the youngster engaging in normal sexual behavior which includes masturbation and sexual curiosity for both girls and boys. In those cases such as the one presented above, counseling is important if the child is to overcome feelings and attitudes about sex which can result in great harm in the future. In many cases such an attitude as displayed by Molly's mother is indicative of sexual problems on the part of parents themselves with counseling highly recommended.

Chapter 4

ADOLESCENCE

G ROWING UP HAS never been easy. There are those who insist that doing so is now more difficult than ever before and bring up such terms as *rapid or unprecedented change, uncertainity of the future, alienation, valuelessness, meaninglessness, hopelessness* and other emotionally laden words in describing the last two decades to prove their point. Others argue that growing up is no more difficult now than in preceding generations. While agreeing that times have indeed changed, they maintain that the tasks to be completed in these crucial years remain essentially the same.

While volumes have been written and various viewpoints expounded, most agree that the period of life we refer to as adolescence, while exciting, can be a most difficult time. Someone has said that "Life is just one thing after another." The statement, perhaps uttered in a moment of frustration or disappointment, while an obvious oversimplification, contains a lot of truth. From the cradle to the grave living is one long series of things to which life demands some semblance of adjustment if we are to survive and function as sane or normal human beings. Even retreat into insanity or suicide is an attempt to adjust to a life which is viewed as no longer tolerable.

While problems and adjustment are both inevitable and necessary at all ages, at no age does the demand for change seem so rapid and adjustment so essential as in adolescence. As a result of this rapid change and the demands physically, socially, morally, intellectually and emotionally placed on youth, it is little wonder that this age has been labeled the storm period of life, characterized by turmoil and stress, both internally and externally.

Indeed so disorganized, fragmented and unpredictable are the responses of youth during this period that phrases such as *teenage neurosis, temporary madness* or *transient psychosis* have been used in an attempt to portray the seriousness and trauma which some authorities believe to be characteristic of these years for many.

While the use of such terms as *neurosis, madness* and *psychosis* may be a gross exaggeration of the problems and distress experienced by adolescents, it is an indication of the difficulty in distinguishing between behavior which might be classified as a normal response to developmental problems and behavior which must be classified as psychopathology. So difficult is the problem of diagnosing mental disturbance in adolescence that experts with years of experience in the diagnosis and treatment of the emotionally disturbed are sometimes hard put to distinguish between normal and abnormal behavior in the adolescent years.

Indeed, some have gone so far as to say that psychologists and psychiatrists who work primarily with adults are not equipped to work with adolescents due to the many differences in problems and responses to their problems between the two age groups.

Whether one agrees with the need for such a sharp division or not, it is readily apparent that behavior often viewed as symptomatic of severe disturbance in adults may or may not be indicative of such disturbances in adolescents.

Rapid and unexplainable swings in mood, from a state of extreme lassitude to one of frantic activity would, for example, be viewed with concern in an adult. While still cause for some concern, such behavior could be quite normal in a fourteen-year-old boy.

Likewise, frequent withdrawal and isolation in an adult is often viewed as symptomatic of some emotional problem. On the other hand, a fifteen-year-old girl may be perfectly satisfied to isolate herself in her room for long periods of time listening to the same record over and over or just lying on her bed lost in her fantasies and daydreams for hours at a time.

Other traits or behaviors such as distrust of their elders, suspicion, irritability, obnoxiousness, fluctuation between love and hate for parents, disdain for rules and regulations, rebelliousness and flouting of authority as well as extreme guilt mixed with a seemingly total lack of conscience at other times might well be viewed as indicators of emotional disturbance in adults. Such traits are considerably less cause for worry in adolescents.

The task of distinguishing healthy behavior from unhealthy or normal from abnormal behavior in adolescents admittedly is a difficult one even for mental health professionals. It is even more difficult for parents, teachers or administrators who are usually untrained in the diagnosis and treatment of emotional disorders.

Adolescent behavior, so often viewed as undesirable or unhealthy by parents and teachers, is most often not a symptom or sign of emotional illness. Behavior which we disapprove of or find offensive does not necessarily mean that the individual engaging in such behavior is mentally ill. For example, as undesirable as the use of drugs or alcohol may be in teenagers, most teenagers who indulge in such are not mentally ill.

Impudence, arguing with teachers, rudeness, insolence, lack of interest in school, truancy, rebellion, disdain for rules and regulations, profanity, fighting and destruction of school property, as undesirable as such behavior may be for teachers and parents, may or may not be an indication of mental disorder.

Rebellion against parental authority, usually resulting in hurt or distress for most parents, is one of the most common means utilized by teenagers in their struggle for autonomy and psychological independence. Such rebellion is essential for teenagers if they are to approach adulthood successfully. Painful though it may be for parents, such behavior is usually an indication of a healthy striving for the establishment of one's own identity rather than a symptom of poor mental health.

As difficult as it may be, it is important that both parents and teachers distinguish between behavior referred to above which is healthy and to be encouraged as opposed to that which is indicative of emotional problems. Regrettably, school records are too often monuments to the failure of teachers and school administrators to make such a distinction.

As thousands of students can attest, remarks in their school records by uninformed, though well-intended, teachers, have haunted students throughout their school careers, often creating unfavorable impressions which they find impossible to overcome.

Margie Lynn Gutgold aptly portrays in verse the essence of the students' dilemma in which teachers failed to make such a distinction. Her poem entitled "Ode to an Anecdote," appearing in the *Personnel And Guidance Journal,* is reproduced in part below.

> My teachers say I have no drive;
> they think I'm smart but lazy.
> They keep a record of my files
> that frankly drives me crazy.
>
> They say they're only anecdotes,
> that what they write won't matter.
> But as I start each higher grade
> my folder's getting fatter.
>
> Before they even know me,
> my teachers simply loathe me.
> They must have read those anecdotes;
> the way they act just shows me.
>
> I have a name and number now
> and amply have been rated
> My records have me scarred for life
> because I'm educated.[12]

Although both parents and teachers do err on occasion, possibly causing emotional scars which last for life, they are much more often a source of great help to children in their struggle for good mental health.

The sensitive coach or teacher is frequently the only person to whom students will go with their problems. Sometimes a parent surrogate, the coach can frequently provide his or her players with the support and encouragement needed as they struggle with the many problems of adolescence. A sympathetic listener, a sensitive observer when help is needed, teachers, even when lacking in the formal training of diagnosing or treating emotional problems, have a great impact on their students. Parents, often the only adults privileged to see their child in situations in which strange or unusual behavior is evident, often feel incapable or unwilling to suggest that all is not well with their child.

It is hoped that the following cases will be of help to parents and teachers faced with the necessity of making decisions and recommendations concerning the mental health of young boys and girls who will someday, hopefully, become healthy young men and women.

Buffy

Buffy, a seventeen-year-old junior, came to the mental health clinic at the insistence of her parents after she had just undergone her second abortion in sixteen months. Slightly obese with an attractive face and pleasant disposition, Buffy stated that she had had sexual intercourse with at least twenty-five or thirty boys since the ninth grade. Stating that she received no pleasure from intercourse, she added that she had sex because it was what her dates wanted and expected. On the occasions when she had said no they usually did not call again.

Convinced that she could attract a male only if she went to bed with him, she had acquired the reputation of an "easy lay." As a result of conversations overheard and fingers pointed at her as she walked across campus, she revealed that she had cried herself to sleep many nights for the past two years.

Despite her unhappiness, however, she had continued to give in even when she did not want to whenever her boyfriends asked her to have sex. A regular church goer with strong religious beliefs, her sexual behavior caused her considerable guilt. Even this did not deter her, however, once sexual pressure was applied again.

Her parents, at first embarrassed and later incensed by her sexual escapades, had tried everything they knew. In anger her father had called her a whore the night before and shouted that she could either "stop screwing everything in pants or leave home for good." It was at this point that her mother, though equally upset, had intervened and arranged for Buffy's appointment at the mental health clinic.

Discussion

Girls who are sexually active to the point described in Buffy's case are frequently deprived in some way. They usually see themselves as lacking in the skills necessary to cope successfully with males in their life and go to great extremes to compensate for the perceived inadequacies. Often feeling that sex is all they have to offer, they move from male to male, usually with the same poor results. Already possessed with a poor concept of themselves, their promiscuous behavior only serves to make them feel even more worthless.

Despite the myths propogated to the contrary, most young females of Buffy's age are neither eager nor ready to enter a sexual relationship, even when the relationship is a good one. The chances of self-enhancement, growth and satisfaction are almost nil under the conditions described above.

If Buffy's promiscuity is not enough to alert one to the presence of emotional problems, then her abortions should. While one abortion is usually traumatic in itself, two abortions in sixteen months are even more significant. Since abortions are serious matters for most young girls, something is usually wrong when they engage in the same behavior which has caused them grief again and again.

It is not our purpose to debate the moral issues involved in abortion. It should be said, however, that whether we agree in principle or not, the fact remains that abortions are now legal and performed by the thousands each year. Most teachers and others in the helping professions will at some time or other be confronted with some young woman who has undergone an abortion. At such times the victim will need all the help and support she can get. Rather than moralizing or preaching to the young woman, sexual excesses such as in Buffy's case should be viewed as just another way in which emotional problems are manifested and thus treated as any other recognizable plea for help.

Alfie

Alfie came to the mental health center after being picked up the previous night by the police for peeping in a neighbor's window. Sixteen years of age, Alfie stated that he had been engaging in such behavior since he was fourteen. He had been caught on several occasions but had never been involved with the police until the night before.

Alfie admitted that he had been looking in the window of an attractive woman several doors from his home, watching her undress for bed. Hearing a noise outside, her husband had called the police who found Alfie still on the front porch when they arrived. After his parents were called in it was agreed that charges would not be pressed if Alfie would agree to see someone for counseling.

In the second session Alfie revealed that he had on occasion also exposed himself to females. Though he did so deliberately, he usually made it appear accidental, like undressing with his window shades up in full view of his next door neighbor. On one occasion in a local park he had stepped from behind some bushes with his trousers open when he saw a young girl approaching.

When questioned about his dating habits Alfie indicated that he had only had three dates in his life. Although interested in girls he said that he had difficulty in relating to them and found it very hard to ask one out.

After three sessions Alfie failed to show up for his fourth appointment. Contacted by the counselor, he came sporadically thereafter but admitted that he came only because he was required to do so. He eventually terminated the sessions with little change evident.

Discussion

Although there are exceptions, Alfie's case is an example illustrating that you cannot require someone to seek counseling and expect it to be very effective. Although his problems were such that psychiatric help was indicated, there is little that can be accomplished when the person is unwilling to work on his problem.

Despite the lack of progress reported in Alfie's case, behavior such as exposing one's self sexually, sneaking around at night looking in windows, dressing in women's clothes by males, etc., is usually cause for psychological referral.

It should be emphasized, however, that the desire to look at nude females on the part of young males should be distinguished from the extremes described above in discussing psychopathology. Most young males find the nude female body stimulating. Such interest accounts for the popularity of girlie magazines with young males. Males probably go to pools and beaches to look as much as to swim. If such behavior were indicative of psychopathology, then most males would have to be classified as mentally ill. This is obviously an exaggeration.

Although Alfie's behavior suggests that his sexual development has been arrested, such individuals are usually not apt to harm others physically as is frequently feared. Although there are exceptions, they are usually shy and timid individuals who have strong doubts about themselves and their sexuality. Girls seldom engage in such behavior. When they are the victims of such acts by males, the psychological damage is usually minimal unless the irate parents make a big issue of the incident.

Although these boys may not be dangerous, their grossly inappropriate sexual conduct (as with Buffy) is still another way of asking, in an indirect fashion, for help. Referral for psychiatric help rather than punishment will certainly be more beneficial to the individual and for society in the long run.

Herb

Herb, a seventeen-year-old senior, was referred to Mr. Brooks, the school counselor, by the principal for fighting in the school cafeteria. A dashing, handsome young male with a devil-may-care attitude, Herb talked of his lack of interest in school and his many conflicts with teachers and other students. Though courteous and polite, he informed Mr. Brooks after approximately thirty minutes that he did not feel that he needed counseling but agreed to stop by again sometime the next week to shoot the breeze.

From talking with the principal and Herb's teachers the next day Mr. Brooks discovered that Herb had been in numerous fights since he entered high school. Dispite his popularity with both boys and girls, he had already acquired the reputation in the community as a person who liked adventure and often went to taverns looking for trouble.

By age seventeen he had already been involved in several motorcycle and car accidents. He was noted for his reckless and fast driving habits and had been arrested twice for drunken driving.

A good athlete, he had played football with the same reckless abandon, with many injuries resulting, however he had quit the team in the eleventh grade.

A review of his earlier school records revealed that Herb had been accident-prone even in the elementary grades. He had several accidents on his bicycle and seemed to always have his arm or leg in a cast or sling. While concerned about their son, Herb's parents had commented to the principal when he tried to talk with them about Herb that he had always been accident-prone but had managed with good luck and the help of the good Lord to survive.

In weeks preceding his visit to see Mr. Brooks, Herb had also begun to skip school, missing at least two days each week. Obviously very intelligent, he approached his school work with the same *don't care* attitude reserved for his extracurricular activities. When several of his teachers had tried to talk with him about his work, he had in his usual good-natured fashion demonstrated a total lack of interest or concern.

A big hit with the girls in his classes, they were delighted with his many daring feats. He loved to drag race and took many a tumble on his motorcycle riding recklessly on back trails and mountains.

When Herb failed to keep his appointment with Mr. Brooks as promised, Mr. Brooks stopped him in the hall and suggested he schedule another appointment. Again Herb indicated that he did not need counseling and refused to schedule an appointment. Hearing that Herb had dropped out of school two weeks later, Mr. Brooks heard nothing else about Herb until several months later when he read in the local paper that Herb had been killed while trying to outrun the police. Shortly before the accident Herb had been seen in a tavern with two of his buddies drinking beer.

Discussion

Some people seem bent on self-destruction. However, if you were to suggest such, most would vehemently deny any intentions of killing themselves. As tragic as Herb's death was, it should come as no great surprise if his previous behavior is examined. Unfortunately, we too often dismiss such reckless and self-destructive activities with the comment that "He is accident prone" or "He is just all boy."

While exciting to watch, often the envy of their classmates, such bravado frequently masks a deep disenchantment with life. Individuals like Herb who sometimes seem not to have a care in the world are often very insecure with a very negative image of themselves despite the confidence they exude. Their seeming lack of fear may well be a cover-up for their self-destructive tendencies, and their constant quest for excitement and adventure an indication of their boredom and meaninglessness in life.

While such individuals may be admired, their frequent risk-taking behavior should not be ignored as a possible warning sign of emotional problems of a serious nature. After all, there are many ways of commiting suicide, but in the end the results are the same as if the person had killed himself with a gun or taken an overdose of sleeping pills. While they are less dramatic, the person who overeats, drinks too much, takes drugs, smokes or engages in behavior continuously which is definitely a hazard to one's health may be just as intent on self-destruction as the person who intentionally drives his car into a tree. It only takes a little longer.

Tanya

Tanya, a seventeen-year-old junior girl from an upper middle-class family was first seen in the mental health clinic after she had been picked up for possession of and selling marijuana.

One of the conditions for her probation was that she seek counseling. When interviewed she seemed contrite and sincerely interested in working on her problems. However, after the second session she failed to show up for the next two appointments. It was only at her probation officer's insistence that she returned for her third session.

From her parole officer it was learned that Tanya had been in trouble on numerous occasions since age thirteen. At that time she had begun to skip school and had begun smoking, much to her parents dismay. She was often in trouble with her teachers for lying, which she did facilely and with little guilt, even when caught in the act by teachers.

She was carried home drunk on several occasions by friends before she was fourteen. At age fifteen she had been caught shoplifting on two occasions and had begun to forge her parent's names on checks shortly afterwards. At age sixteen she had stolen her grandfather's car and run away from home for two days. She was returned by police after she had wrecked the car in a nearby town.

In each of the above situations her parents or grandparents had rushed to her defense, either refusing to press charges or paying the stores for the merchandise she had taken. Other than pointing out the immorality of her behavior, the parents did nothing.

With Tanya's permission it was learned from her high school counselor that she had also frequently been in trouble in school with peers as well as teachers and administrators.

A very pretty girl, she seemed to take great delight in dating her classmates' boyfriends. After having sexual relations with them, which she made known to their girlfriends, she usually dropped them. She had by her own admission never been deeply involved with anyone.

At age seventeen she had begun dating older men, usually of questionable character and certainly not the sort her parents had envisioned her dating and eventually marrying. While seventeen she had become pregnant and had an abortion. By this time she was using drugs in addition to alcohol to the point that her parents became alarmed, realizing for the first time that their daughter's behavior could no longer be ignored. They had half-heartedly encouraged her to talk with the school counselor on several occasions before. She would usually go for one or two sessions, not to return again until her parents or teachers insisted that she do so after becoming involved in another of her numerous escapades.

When she did show up for the appointments she usually did so with no outward sign of anxiety or remorse. For the most part she seemed to feel that she had done nothing wrong. As if entirely void of feelings or conscience, she would return in a few days or weeks accused of doing the same sort of things which had gotten her in trouble earlier. Never seeming to profit from previous experiences, she displayed no desire to change at all. Seemingly indifferent to all rules and regulations, she appeared to march to a different drummer altogether. Obviously intelligent and glib of tongue, she was often able to talk herself out of situations for which other students would have been dealt with more severely.

Despite her many difficulties, she was still liked by both peers and teachers, although she never allowed anyone to get very close to her.

With no great change apparent, although she did remain relatively free of trouble during the period, Tanya immediately ceased coming for counseling when she was no longer required to do so.

Just before graduation she dropped out of school and married an older man known to have a severe drug problem.

Discussion

All children and adolescents fantasize and engage in behavior which is socially unacceptable at times. Most manage to break rules and regulations and go through periods of rebellion in which they seem to take great pleasure in being stubborn, disagreeable and independent of parents, teachers and others in positions of authority. Such behavior usually generates some degree of anger and unhappiness on the part of parents and teachers. In most cases this is part of the developmental process we refer to as growing up and should not be interpreted as a sign of mental illness.

In Tanya's case, however, her behavior suggests that her pattern of relating to others is more than just a stage of rebellion which most young people go through at some time or other. Her behavior seems instead to be more indicative of a pattern begun in childhood which developed into a permanent life-style as she grew older. Such individuals quite often turn out to be juvenile delinquents or chronic offenders in society as adults. Many end up in prison. If they do manage to escape imprisonment they are frequently involved in drugs, alcohol, prostitution or some other unlawful activity. No matter how much they are reprimanded, punished, cajoled or prayed for by frantic and concerned parents, they seem unable or unwilling to change. They seem unable to profit from previous mistakes or experiences. They may engage in unlawful acts with no display of guilt or conscience. They are often able to talk themselves out of situations when they are caught. They may be convincing liars and sometimes appear repentant in order to escape prosecution or punishment. Often attractive and intelligent, they frequently put up a good front to fool others or to take advantage of them.

While most students at times engage in behavior or display symptoms mentioned below, teachers and parents should be alert to the possibility of a more serious problem when these or similar symptoms occur with *frequency*. Referral to a mental health professional for evaluation should be suggested if the student

1. Takes advantage of others frequently with no concern for the other's welfare
2. Frequently lies, steals, cheats or engages in activities which would arouse guilt or awareness of wrongdoing in others with no display of remorse or conscience
3. Seems unable to learn from previous mistakes or experiences and repeats behavior which has caused him trouble before
4. Tends to blame others for his behavior
5. Is immature or impulsive beyond what is usually expected of others in the same age group
6. Rebels against all authority
7. Has poor relationships with others

8. Appears sorry and contrite when caught in some misdeed, promising to change, only to repeat unacceptable behavior again

9. Refuses to live by any code of morals or ethics

10. Is extremely self-centered, concerned only with getting what he wants right now with no ability to postpone gratification

11. Refuses to accept any responsibility for his behavior or to look ahead to the consequences which might be expected to occur.

Of all emotional problems encountered by teachers there is perhaps nothing more frustrating than a student suffering from the problem described above. It is frustrating and discouraging for the simple reason that no matter how much effort or concern is expended, the student often fails to respond with any noticeable or positive change.

It should at this point be emphasized that individuals with problems similar to Tanya's are the exception when it comes to treatment and prognosis in emotional disorders. Fortunately, most emotional problems are highly treatable, and in recent years special therapeutic programs have reported greater success in treating problems similar to those suffered by Tanya than had been previously reported. In any event, referral for professional help is usually advisable with the cooperation of parents, teachers and others needed if relief in any form is to be expected.

Jan

Ms. Abrams first became concerned with Jan, a sixteen-year-old student, when she began crying uncontrollably during math class after giving the wrong answer to a question.

Mystified by Jan's reaction since she had not scolded or tried to embarrass her in any way, Ms. Abrams asked her to remain after school. With considerable effort, Jan managed to discuss her fear of failing math for the semester. Aware that Jan was one of her better students, Ms. Abrams attempted to reassure Jan that she was in no danger of failing by showing her her test grades for the course. Although she had a 95 average, Jan's fear of failure remained.

Describing herself as a born worrier, Jan then began to share with Ms. Abrams her feeling that she was always under great pressure to make A's in all her classes. She admitted that most of the pressure came from within and that her parents had repeatedly tried to get her to study less and enjoy life more. On an earlier occasion they had hidden her books for several weeks to keep her from studying. Instead of relaxing, however, Jan stated that she almost went crazy looking for her books.

Although she always made top grades and turned in her work on time, she complained that her teachers were not very understanding and just kept piling the work on. She said that she had been extremely tense for the past week since midterm exams were approaching. She had also been having such severe headaches that when she went home in the afternoon she would fall on her bed and scream. Her headaches seemed to worsen when she sat down and tried to study. She also complained of tension in the back of her neck as well as stomach pains and wondered if she might not have an ulcer.

At Ms. Abrams' suggestion, Jan agreed to see the school counselor the following morning. In the several sessions that followed he learned that Jan, from her earliest years, had been a very tense and conscientious person who seemed to be unable to relax and enjoy herself. If she made an A on an exam she worried because she had not made an A+.

A firm believer in organization, she indicated that even as a child she had operated on a rigid schedule. While in the first grade, before retiring at night, she would make out her schedule for the next day to the smallest detail, beginning at seven when she got up until nine when she went to bed. If she let herself be persuaded into taking a trip or taking a day off, she reported that she could never enjoy herself owing to her guilt and the feeling that she ought to be studying.

Not only did she worry about not living up to her own high standards, she also worried constantly that she would disappoint her parents, teachers, relatives and friends. She also worried about her mother's health and was fearful that her mother would some day have a nervous breakdown, which, in her thinking, would be largely Jan's fault. On those rare occasions when she dated she refused to do anything without first consulting her mother, which drove her boyfriend to distraction.

Her need for order and structure seemed to permeate most areas of her life. If, for example, she noticed picture frames at a slight tilt or if she saw books out of line on bookshelves, it made her uncomfortable. At the first opportunity she would set them straight. Otherwise she remained anxious.

After several visits to the counselor's office Jan informed him that she would not return since she could not take the time from her studies necessary for the appointments.

Discussion

Most adolescents experience adjustment problems. They are often quite concerned with failure or success in school, peer approval and living up to parental expectations. They are also apt to be moody, self-conscious and lacking in self-confidence in many situations.

In Jan's case, however, she seemed to have an unusually high need for approval as evidenced by her reluctance to do anything without first seeking parental consent. Ignoring or failing to trust her own judgment in almost every case, she seemed to live solely for the approval of others. Her need to conform to the expectations she perceived others to have of her was also excessive. Her life seemed dominated by shoulds and oughts. She was overly conscientious and rigid to the degree that if her schedule was disrupted she found it almost unbearable.

One of the most disturbing qualities was her inability to relax and enjoy herself without feeling exceedingly guilty. While many individuals experience a desire to straighten a crooked picture or rearrange books which are out of order, Jan's need to do so was grossly out of proportion.

As with any physical complaint, Jan's headaches and stomach pains should be discussed with a physician. It should never be assumed by any nonmedical person that physical problems are all in one's head. Whatever the cause, it is nature's way of reminding us that something is wrong. In Jan's case it might well be her body's way of telling her to slow down.

As demonstrated by Jan, such people are often hard to work with in a counseling setting and frequently insist that they are unable to slow down or quit worrying even when they are convinced that their behavior is detrimental to their health. Regardless of the frustration in trying to counsel with such individuals, it is important that the effort be made due to the potential for even more serious emotional problems in the years ahead.

Finally, youngsters like Jan are particularly in jeopardy as they appear so good and so readily win compliments from parents and teachers. They tend to be signaled out as ideal children and adolescents when in fact they should be signaled out as *too* good and *too* conforming.

Vic

Vic, a handsome seventeen-year-old junior, had been seen in the emergency room of the local hospital after taking all the pills he could find in the family medicine cabinet. After some hours in which the outcome had been doubtful, he was admitted for observation to the hospital. Interviewed by a member of the mental health staff, Vic had admitted that his only regret was that he had been unsuccessful in killing himself and that he would do a better job next time. Released to the care of his parents several days later, Vic reluctantly agreed to return for counseling on an outpatient basis.

In the first sessions, it was learned that Vic had been diagnosed as having rheumatic fever when he was eleven years old. Aspiring to be a baseball player, he had become discouraged when he had been unable to compete with the other boys in the weekly softball games at the local YMCA. Turning to music, where he discovered that he had considerable talent, he had learned to play the guitar and sing. He had done so well that he was in great demand for social and church functions in the community. Two years later he and several other students had formed a band which had also proved to be a success.

Later, however, bothered by pains in his hands and shoulders, he had been told by his physician that he had a form of arthritis which might become progressively worse. Even by this time he had already begun to experience some stiffness in his hands and fingers. In the morning his fingers were often stiff and painful with the result that he began having difficulty playing guitar. Convinced that nature had again played a cruel joke on him, he became more and more depressed when he thought of having to give up his music.

Complaining to his girlfriend so much that she threatened to break up with him unless he quit feeling so sorry for himself, he continued nonetheless to be depressed and bitter in her presence. On numerous occasions he said that he would be better off if he had not been born. At other times he would in a more direct manner indicate that he was seriously thinking of killing himself. Thinking that she might jar him out of his self-pity, Sue had told him to go ahead and do it or quit talking about it so much. Later that same evening Vic had been found unconscious in his bedroom by his parents and rushed to the hospital near death.

Discussion

In regard to Vic's physical problems it should be emphasized that any illness which incapacitates or restricts normal functioning is also apt to create emotional problems of acceptance and adjustment. Chronic diseases, which usually give rise to anxiety and depression, especially when there is no definite cure, may include such disorders as arthritis, hypoglycemia, diabetes, asthma and epilepsy.

Despite the absence of any absolute cure, both parents and children should recognize that with proper medical care many of these individuals can lead normal lives, some completely symptom-free. Even for those in whom disease control is more difficult there is always the hope that medical science will someday bring relief or a cure.

In any event we cannot stress too strongly the importance of parental attitudes in the handling of any chronic disorder such as diabetes, epilepsy or arthritis. If the parent feels that some stigma is attached to such a disorder or that the child is something less than a whole person, this will in all likelihood be communicated to the child.

In all cases the child's doctor should be consulted and in most cases, unless medically contraindicated, the child should be encouraged to live a life as near normal as possible. Too often the child is crippled more by parental attitudes such as overprotectiveness than by the illness itself.

In most cases where chronic physical disorders exist both parent and child can profit from counseling. While care of the body is of considerable importance, the patient's emotions should never be ignored in the treatment of diseases which will require drastic alterations in life-style. If counseling had been possible for Vic, chances are that he would have come up with a different solution to his problem.

As for Vic's attempt to kill himself, it is easy to understand, in view of his condition and sense of frustration, why he might be tempted to pursue such a course. In Vic's case Sue made the mistake many individuals do whenever suicide becomes an issue. Believing as many do that people who talk about suicide never follow through with their threats to kill themselves, Sue had dared him to do just that. Already despondent with an increasing sense of physical loss and vocational failure, Vic probably interpreted Sue's behavior as a lack of concern and final proof that life was for him not worth the effort.

Even in cases where threats of suicide are used for the purpose of emotional blackmail, such threats should never be ignored. For the nonprofessional involved with a person talking about suicide such threats should be viewed as reason for referral to someone who is trained to evaluate the seriousness of such threats. Contrary to what many believe, research has shown that most individuals who have killed themselves or made a serious attempt to do so have communicated in various ways their intentions beforehand. A large number have consulted with physicians while others have talked to associates, family, clergymen or mental health professionals.

The decision to kill one's self is usually not a sudden one.

Suicide is usually attempted only after the individual feels that he has exhausted all other means of facing life or his problems. In most cases it is a deliberate act planned for weeks or months in advance. Some will save up medicine or go to great lengths to plan their demise. In rarer cases the severely disturbed individual, out of contact with reality or incapable of assuming responsibility for his actions, will act quickly and impulsively without warning. Most, however, communicate in various ways beforehand their intentions of doing harm to themselves.

Although it is believed that suicide is on the increase among children and students, there is no way of determining just how many do actually make attempts. Accuracy regarding the number who succeed is even more difficult for obvious reasons. Many authorities suggest that many deaths which are ruled accidental may in truth be suicides. In other cases, in order to prevent embarrassment for families of victims, mention of the word *suicide* is avoided, even when there is good reason to suspect that suicide is the cause of death.

As for assessing the potential for suicide in children and young people, mental health assistance should be sought if the child or student

1. Is severely depressed or shows other signs of emotional distress or mental illness which would suggest that he is not capable of assuming responsibility for himself.

2. Talks of suicide or expresses in more subtle ways his intention of killing himself. Parents and teachers should be alerted, for example, if the child makes such statements as "I may not be around much longer," "You won't be bothered with me anymore," or "The world would be better off without me," etc.

3. Has attempted suicide before.

4. Has developed a specific plan to kill himself. Individuals who have planned their deaths to the point of collecting pills, buying a gun or writing a note may be more apt to follow through with the act than is the person who casually thinks about suicide.

5. Remains depressed even after counseling or other treat-

ment has been undertaken.

6. Uses drugs or alcohol extensively.

7. Remains depressed over the loss of a significant figure in their life for a long period of time.

8. Feels that all is hopeless and that things will never get better.

9. Takes unnecessary risks or engages in behavior frequently of a self-destructive nature, i.e. repeated auto accidents, numerous physical injuries; careless indulgence in sky diving, auto racing, heavy use of drugs, cigarettes, alcohol, etc.

10. Suddenly appears to be calm or significantly less depressed.

Experts on suicide tell us that we should be very cautious at this point, for such a change may indicate that a suicidal decision has been made and the person is now resigned to his fate. Another crucial time is when the depression begins to lift. Again the experts warn us that while severely depressed, the person may be too immobilized to find the energy to destroy himself. As he becomes less depressed, however, he may now be able to mobilize the energy necessary to carry out the act.

Gale

Gale, an eighteen-year-old senior at a girls' boarding school, opened her first session with Ms. Jones, the counselor, with the statement that she had lost all her motivation to do her school work and wondered if Ms. Jones could do something to help her regain her desire to study. She followed this by saying that she was about to go crazy and had been seriously considering killing herself. Speaking and moving with great effort, she sat in silence for long periods of time. She spoke only when questioned or urged to do so by Ms. Jones. She appeared to be frightened, with her gaze fixed on the floor. She rarely looked at Ms. Jones even when talking. Complaining of being depressed, she said she wanted to stay in her room and sleep most of the time. In the last two weeks she had been averaging fourteen hours of sleep per day. Each day when she left class she would go to her room and sleep. She sometimes skipped dinner, sleeping until the following morning. Even then she had difficulty getting up in the morning. Denying that she had ever attempted suicide before, she said that she had thought of it frequently and had been considering it even more seriously and often in recent weeks.

With great effort, Ms. Jones was able to learn that Gale's father had died when she was fourteen. In response to her questions, Gale revealed that she had had mixed emotions about his death. Never very close to him, she had been upset when he died, but had also experienced feelings of anger mixed with relief. Her mother, an alcoholic, was also prone to depression. Shortly after her father's death Gale's mother placed her in the private boarding school.

With no change in expression, she volunteered the information that she wished her mother would die also. Seemingly very resentful of the intrusion, Gale indicated that her mother would call periodically, complaining of being alone and beg Gale to come home for a visit. To avoid feelings of guilt, Gale would go despite the fact that she hated going since her mother was usually drunk. At the end of most visits both usually ended up feeling even worse about themselves and their relationship.

Admitting that she would like to be a hermit, Gale indicated that she could tolerate people only when she had been smoking pot. In the last month, however, even this had not worked and she had given up smoking.

Regarding her relationship with the other girls, Gale revealed that she seldom associated with them. Most of the other girls would gather in the large living room each evening to talk or engage in other activities. Describing this as one of the most difficult times of the day for her, Gale confessed that she would usually slip down the hall without stopping in on the way to her room. Once in her room she would either sleep or busy herself rearranging the furniture in her room which she did several times each week. She had discovered a place on the roof which was accessible from her bedroom window to which she could escape if the pressure to participate in activities with the other girls became too intense.

Describing her relationship with boys, Gale said that she

always felt as if they were after her only for sex. A very attractive girl, she had numerous opportunities to date but seldom accepted. She had had sexual intercourse with several different boys but indicated that she had never enjoyed intercourse and only did it because she found it difficult to say no. If anyone, male or female, tried to get close, she would retreat.

The only visible sign of feeling displayed in the session occurred when Gale began to discuss the death of her cat two weeks earlier. Attributing her most recent state of depression to his death, Gale stated that he was the only friend she had.

Revealing her fondness for plants and flowers, Gale then talked in her slow and tired way at some length of her desire to major in horticulture when she went to college. She gave as her reason for wanting to work with plants her difficulty in trusting and relating to humans, indicating that she could get along well with plants.

Concluding the session by again asking for help with her lack of motivation, Gale agreed to schedule another appointment with Ms. Jones. However, she failed to keep the appointment. Concerned about her, Ms. Jones contacted Gale, and another appointment was scheduled which Gale also failed to keep. Two weeks later she graduated without being seen again for counseling.

Discussion

There are a number of reasons to be disturbed by Gale's behavior and emotional state. The most immediate concern is obviously her depression and the threat of suicide. As stated earlier, talk of doing harm to one's self should never be ignored. Whether it is intended or just an attempt to get help or attention, the matter of suicide should be explored thoroughly rather than avoided. Gale's need to sleep for long periods of time, her general demeanor, stuporous or trance-like states, her lethargy and loss of interest and motivation are all suggestive of a rather deep depression and should be treated immediately.

There were also many obvious and unresolved feelings about the death of her father with which Gale needed to deal. Feelings similar to those experienced by Gale are quite common whenever one is confronted with death, especially when the relationship has not been a good one as in the case of Gale and her father. Even if the relationship has been a good one, many children experience strong feelings of anger and frustration toward the dead parent. They may even view the death as a form of abandonment.

Gale's relationship with her mother is also reason for concern. Her mother's alcoholism and emotional state would suggest that Gale's family life has probably been very chaotic with the absence of any healthy role model to guide her in the important and formative years of her life.

From a long-range viewpoint her difficulty in human relationships is the most disturbing trait or characteristic mentioned above. While there are many normal and well-adjusted people who enjoy the company of animals and working with plants, few go to the extreme that Gale did in substituting such activities and relationships for human contact.

Her statement that she could only relate to other human beings while smoking pot is further indication that she is experiencing some severe difficulties in this area. Any individual who must use alcohol, smoke pot or engage in the use of some other drug in order to feel comfortable in a social situation should be considered a possible candidate for more severe problems in the future.

Gale's attitudes toward males in general and in sexual matters in particular are further evidence that her difficulties in the field of interpersonal relationships were rather extensive.

In addition, her feelings that she was about to go crazy, the extreme measures she took to escape, and the constant rearranging of her furniture (which suggests severe anxiety and disappointment with her environment) are reasons to suggest psychiatric help.

Without this sort of intervention Gale will most probably continue to experience mental distress with even more drastic emotional difficulties likely. In all probability Gale was showing signs of emotional problems long before her senior year. It is most unfortunate that this behavior went undetected or untreated for so long. Had treatment been initiated earlier, her chances for a happier life would have been increased.

Jo

Jo, a pretty seventeen-year-old junior, dropped by Mr. Ames' office to talk with him about having to leave his chemistry class the day before in the middle of his lecture. After apologizing profusely she began to discuss the fear she had that she was going to faint while in his class. Although she began to feel giddy and lightheaded at the beginning of the class, she had managed to keep the feeling under control for the first half of his lecture. She insisted, however, that she had eventually felt so dizzy that she was convinced that she had to get out of the room or else faint. Experiencing some nausea and shortness of breath along with the dizziness, she had rushed from the room to the girl's lounge where she washed her face before going outside the building. After some moments she had felt well enough to go to the office and call her parents to come and get her. On the day of her visit to Mr. Ames' office, she had again experienced some of the same feelings but had managed to convince herself that she would be all right and remained for the entire period.

Thinking she might have a virus which had been going around, Mr. Ames suggested that Jo see her family physician. At this point Jo informed him that she was certain that her attacks were not due to any virus although she suspected they might be caused by something more serious. She then indicated that she had been having similar attacks for over a year, however, they had become more frequent in recent weeks. Some months before she had talked with her family doctor about her attacks. After giving her a thorough physical examination the doctor had informed her that he could find no organic cause for her attacks and suggested that it might be her nerves.

After talking with her physician and being reassured that she was not seriously ill, Jo stated that the attacks stopped for about two months. However they had returned and gradually increased in frequency. These attacks seemed to occur without any obvious reason, even when she was driving her car on the freeway or eating in a restaurant. On two occasions they had occurred while she was driving over a high bridge. On other occasions they had occurred at ball games and once while she was in church.

In most cases the attacks seemed to follow a pattern. She would be enjoying herself with no obvious concerns at the moment when all at once she would begin to feel uneasy with the feeling that something bad was about to happen. She usually then began to feel dizzy or faint. If she struggled against the feelings and could convince herself that she was going to be okay, she could often contain her feelings. On other occasions, however, she would have to pull her car over to the side of the road or leave the restaurant in a panic lest she pass out completely. Questioning revealed however she had in fact never passed out.

Aware that Jo was one of his better and more conscientious students, Mr. Ames encouraged her to return to talk with him further the next afternoon. During the second meeting he learned that Jo was also unable to sleep at night due to thoughts of death. At other times she would wake up in the morning with death on her mind and find herself unable to rid herself of such thoughts for the rest of the day. When talking of the future, she revealed that even if she lived she always expected the worst.

Although he had noticed that Jo appeared to be a worrier and was often tense and uptight, he was surprised to hear her describe herself and her future in such pessimistic terms. By now convinced that Jo's problems were deeper than he had first suspected, he suggested that she see the school psychologist to discuss her feelings further.

Discussion

Everyone experiences fear and anxiety. A life totally free of anxiety is neither possible nor desirable for the simple reason that anxiety can serve as an impetus for creative and beneficial activities. While it can be beneficial, in excess it can also be a deterrent to healthy functioning and even crippling in the more severe cases. For this reason it is important to distinguish between reasonable fear and anxiety, and anxiety of the proportion experienced by Jo.

Jo's anxiety, sometimes referred to as free floating anxiety, cannot usually be traced to any particular situation or event as the precipitating cause. It is often a vague, sometimes overwhelming sense that something is wrong or that something catastrophic is about to happen. It may vary in intensity from a mild feeling of discomfort to a full blown panic state in which the individual is completely disabled, unable to function, or even out of contact with reality to the point that the person and the environment seem unreal.

Individuals prone to such episodes of generalized uncontrollable fear or anxiety are often described as chronic worriers who are never able to relax. They may be preoccupied with thoughts of dying or always expecting something bad to happen. They may have difficulty sleeping or have frequent nightmares when they are able to sleep. They may seem unduly tense while driving, working, playing or studying. When anxious they may complain of heart palpitations, excessive sweating, difficulty in breathing, swallowing or walking. They may frequently feel as if they are going to faint, even die. Complaints of dry mouth and throat, even to the point of choking, are quite common.

Such feelings may be chronic or acute. In the more serious or troublesome cases medication may be required. The person suffering from such attacks may become infuriated when observers laugh at his fear or tell him the trouble is only in his head. To the person troubled by such episodes they are no laughing matter.

While some students manage to tolerate or live with their anxieties, referral to a psychiatrist or other mental health professional is strongly recommended when the anxiety approaches the level described above. While medication or short-term therapy can often provide relief, more intensive therapy is usually necessary or desirable. As in other cases in which physical symptoms are described, referral to a medically trained practitioner is very important.

Bobby

Bobby, a sixteen-year-old sophomore of slender build, entered the school counselor's office for the first time after a week's absence from school.

Volunteering the information that he had been sick with the flu, Bobby refused to discuss his illness any further. During the session he was obviously anxious. He wet his lips frequently, sighed deeply and on occasions took in great gulps of air as if he were having difficulty breathing. Squirming uncomfortably in his chair and asking for water on two occasions, he made several attempts to speak about his reasons for scheduling the appointment. Opening his mouth as if about to speak it seemed as though the words were stuck in his throat. Though his lips moved no sound came forth. After twenty minutes he expressed a desire to leave, indicating that he had never been able to discuss his problem with anyone.

Three days later Bobby again returned for another appointment. After going through many of the same motions for about thirty minutes, he was able to tell Mr. James that he had not really had the flu but had been in the intensive care unit at a local hospital for two days after taking a bottle of aspirin in an attempt to kill himself. Although he talked at some length of his suicide attempt, he was still unable to tell Mr. James why he had tried to kill himself. Even his parents did not know.

During a third appointment, Bobby began by saying that he just had to talk to someone about his problem since he could no longer handle it by himself. He then blurted out, "I think I am queer." After speaking, he then remained silent for several moments, seemingly relieved that he had finally been able to reveal his fear to someone else, but at the same time embarrassed and troubled by such an admission.

In response to the counselor's question as to his feelings, Bobby, with great intensity, said he could not bear the thought of being homosexual and that it went against everything he believed in. Hoping to marry and have a family someday, he was afraid that such would never come about.

He was especially concerned lest his parents discover that he had such thoughts. His father would never be able to accept his only son as a homosexual. An outdoorsman who enjoyed athletics, his father had hoped that his son would follow in his steps. Although he had never said so, Bobby was convinced that his father had been disappointed that he had not been involved in football and baseball. Indicating that he had never been good enough to compete with the other boys in these areas, Bobby spoke with some pride of his gymnastic skills, however these had not been emphasized in his school and he had received little in the way of training or recognition as a result.

Denying that he had ever had any homosexual experiences, Bobby said he had been approached by several males in the past two years. Although he had been tempted, he had refused their invitations. One of these boys had told him that he looked like the type who would enjoy sex with another boy. Although he had experienced doubts about his sexuality before, this comment had aroused real doubts which he had, up to now, managed to push aside.

Getting along well with girls, he spent a lot of time with them and went out on dates frequently. He insisted, however, that he never received any pleasure or had any desire to become involved physically with any of the girls he dated. When he did force himself to kiss a girl occasionally, he was never aroused sexually.

Discussing masturbation, which he engaged in several times weekly, he said his fantasies were usually of males rather than females. When he did think of females, they were always having intercourse with some male other than himself.

Referring again to his earlier years, Bobby revealed that though he had tried to enjoy football and baseball, he had never been able to do so. Seeing himself as very uncoordinated when it came to physical activities, he added that his small physique had been a handicap when he tried to play football, wrestle or engage in other feats of strength with male classmates. As a consequence he turned more and more to his books or else sought out young girls for companionship where he felt more accepted.

This pattern had continued throughout his high school years

with few males involved in his daily activities. His only satisfying contacts with males had occurred in his physical science classes where he participated with other boys in science experiments. Because he was an excellent student, they sought him out for assistance.

In other areas like sports, however, they usually ignored him or teased him about his poor performance. When he was forced to participate in these sports, he was always the last one chosen. When he struck out or missed a pop fly his teammates would tell him that he played like a girl or taunt him with cries of sissy pants or some other similar label.

After several sessions with Bobby, Mr. James suggested that he see a psychiatrist because of his unhappiness and his expressed desire to become heterosexual.

Discussion

Most people who have homosexual fantasies or thoughts are not homosexual. Many young people, both male and female, engage in homosexual activities at some time or other without becoming homosexual. To have such thoughts or to engage in such behavior does not mean that the individual is homosexual. Most go on to develop a normal and healthy sexual life-style.

In Bobby's case, however, his sexual fears seem to be based on more than just an occasional or passing concern with homosexual matters. If nothing else, his excessive anxiety about being homosexual, serious enough to prompt him to attempt suicide, would be ample reason to recommend professional help. While suicide is by no means restricted to homosexuals, many individuals who are unable to tolerate the idea of being homosexual or the many frustrations encountered in pursuing such a life-style do entertain or follow through with thoughts of suicide. Consequently, the possibility of suicide should not be ignored.

Whether right or wrong, there are customary roles and expectations in our society which males and females are supposed to follow and live up to. If they fail to do so, there are usually serious reservations about their sexual identity. With females the consequences may not be so severe or critics so vocal as with young males. Whether one is in agreement with the traditional separation of appropriate behavior and activities for the two sexes, the fact remains that such a division does exist and the young boy or girl who deviates from what is expected usually pays a rather steep price, not only in regard to relationships with peers but with adults in society as well.

While there have been some trends and changes in recent years which hopefully will result in less sexual pressure of this sort, the fact remains that for the present many young boys and girls continue to experience emotional and physical trauma in regard to their failure to conform to societal expectations of what is *manly* or *womanly*.

It is important in the formative years of life that young boys have male adult figures to identify with and that young girls have good female adult models. If this is not true within the family, then a surrogate parent can often fulfill this vital function which many coaches and teachers do. In Bobby's case, while it would seem that his father supplied such a role model in the form of a supermasculine father, it is very possible that Bobby was unable to identify with his father for the very reason that he was *too much* of a man and that his expectations of his son were unrealistic. The results were perhaps the same as if he had no male to identify with at all.

Schools and physical education programs too often fall into the same trap with their sometimes unrealistic expectations with rewards going to the more physically gifted. While it may be appropriate to reward excellence of performance in athletics as well as in other endeavors, it is not conducive to the physical, social or mental well-being of those not so gifted to place such individuals in a position in which they learn to perceive of themselves as undesirable or as athletic morons.

There are many other activities for those who cannot excel in basketball or football which can add greatly to their physical growth and development as well as to the development of themselves as adequate young men and women. Since physical accomplishments and athletics play such a major role in our society in evaluating one's worth as male or female, it should be emphasized that the capable coach or athletic director will develop a program in which all can participate and one in which the physical worth of every individual is encouraged and made possible.

There is still no consensus of opinion as to the cause of homosexuality. Whatever the cause, once it is established that the child or adolescent has homosexual inclinations, teachers and parents are usually not prepared to engage in treatment for those who express a desire to change. Such is usually reserved for the therapist with experience and training in the treatment of homosexuality.

Since many therapists themselves do not view homosexuality as a very treatable disorder, it is important that individuals seeking help be referred to a therapist who does believe that change is possible and treatment helpful. There are behavior modification programs which have reported remarkable rates of success in treating homosexuals who want to change. The progress for those who express no desire to change is another matter. In Bobby's case, however, he did seem to be highly motivated toward a heterosexual life-style. With this degree of motivation and at his age the chances are good that he can be helped.

Counseling is usually needed even for those who insist that they prefer the homosexual way of life since it does involve many problems of adjustment and acceptance of themselves.

Whether one approves of homosexuality or not, we are confronted with the fact that many human beings are now more open than ever before in regard to their homosexual feelings and behavior. Due to the efforts of such groups as the Gay Liberation Movement there has developed a more liberal attitude toward homosexuality. While such thinking has probably had a greater impact on adults, students at all age levels have probably been affected as well. As a result of this openness and more lenient attitudes toward homosexuality we can expect to see an increase in problems associated with this behavior in schools and society in general.

Although some psychiatrists disagree, further proof of the changing attitudes in regard to homosexuality is the recent move by the American Psychiatric Association in which homosexuality is no longer classified as mental illness.

Despite the trend toward a more liberal view of sexual practices between those of the same sex, the authors still maintain that the establishment of a satisfying sexual relationship between members of the opposite sex remains *for most* the preferred lifestyle. Assuming that something can be done for those who want to pursue such a way of life, then there are significant warning signs which might alert teachers and parents to the need of certain young people for professional help. Some of these signs are listed below:

1. Difficulty in identifying with or relating to members of one's own sex;

2. Does not develop masculine or feminine interests in keeping with one's own sex;

3. In the case of young boys special attention should be given when peers frequently refer to him as *sissy, queer, fag* or some other term reflecting on his masculinity. While children can be very cruel in such cases they can also be very perceptive, often picking up signals that something is wrong before adults. Even when their taunts are unjustified and without basis, the child subjected to such attacks over an extended period can be expected to suffer severe anxiety. In serious cases such criticism can push a child already having doubts about his sexuality even further down the road toward homosexuality. Since opinions of peers are so important to young people, some may become convinced without basis that something is indeed wrong with them sexually.

4. Develops mannerisms, gestures, ways of speaking, walking or behaving more in keeping with what is usually expected of the opposite sex;

5. In the case of young boys the desire to wear feminine clothing, play with dolls or toys usually associated with girls to the exclusion of male interest or pursuits. In the case of girls such a distinction is more difficult to make due to the widespread acceptance of the wearing of male clothing by females and the participation in sports once played only by males.

6. Extended sexual relationships with members of the same

sex. We include the word *extended* since many, if not most, adolescents engage in some form of sexual experimentation or exploration with members of the same sex.

7. Unusual fear, apathy or avoidance of the opposite sex. Again, caution is urged since it is quite normal for boys and girls to go through a period in which they prefer the company of their own sex, often to the point of going to great lengths to avoid contact with members of the opposite sex.

8. While it is often impossible for teachers to have access to such information or for parents themselves to be objective enough, the relationship between parents and children can often be of great significance in evaluating the potentiality for homosexuality in the child. It is believed by many authorities that homosexual tendencies are more likely to develop if the child's parents are overprotective, seductive, distant or absent. For example, the young boy whose father may be cruel, domineering, passive, rejecting, too busy or cold to the point that any positive identification fails to occur. For the young girl the uncaring, domineering, passive or distant mother may result in difficulty in acceptance of her role as a female.

Since there are so many misconceptions and prejudices regarding homosexuality, we cannot emphasize too strongly that teachers and parents exert great care in the application of the possible warning signals listed above.

It is not unusual, for example, to hear someone say that a homosexual can be identified by such characteristics as dress, body build, lack of athletic skills, body movements, gestures or interest in art, music or the theater. The truth is that there is no simple or single way of describing the homosexual any more than there is any simple or single way of describing the heterosexual.

About the only thing that can be said with certainty is that homosexuals are as different as heterosexuals and include people from all walks of life and of all shapes, sizes and colors. The small uncoordinated artist with long hair and hip huggers may be having a very satisfying heterosexual relationship while a big husky defensive tackle on the high school or pro football team may be engaging in homosexual activities on the weekend.

Finally, it should be stressed that a male can desire a warm and close relationship with another male for many reasons. This does not necessarily mean that he is a homosexual. The girl who becomes anxious because she experiences a sense of warmth or enjoys being around an older woman or teacher may be searching for the warmth she never had from her mother and may have nothing to do with either overt or latent homosexual feelings.

Whatever the case, concerns about homosexuality should not be ignored. For those experiencing anxiety about being homosexual based on incorrect information or ignorance, an explanation or assurance that it is normal to experience certain feelings or desires may be enough to alleviate the anxiety. For those wishing to change their sexual orientation or work with the many problems incumbent on the homosexual in our society, professional help is usually desirable.

Karla

Karla, an attractive seventeen-year-old girl, was brought to the mental health clinic by her mother who immediately informed Mr. West, the counselor, that her daughter was engaging in a homosexual relationship with one of her classmates. Insisting that she would not tolerate such behavior in one of her children, she demanded that something be done for her child.

Asking to speak with Karla alone, Mr. West learned that Karla possessed considerable talent in both art and music. Academically she had done well in school and was an excellent swimmer. In social situations, however, she revealed that she did not feel accepted due primarily to her homosexuality.

In discussing her sexual feelings Karla stated that she had first begun to suspect that she was homosexual when she was fourteen after reading an article in a book about lesbians. It was the first time she had ever heard the word and had never thought of her relationship with Pam in sexual terms or as anything other than something beautiful. From that time on, however, she indicated that she began to see herself as unwholesome and the relationship as something dirty. For the next two years she had cried herself to sleep each night with such thoughts.

Shortly after her discovery about herself she had gone to the school counselor. Much to her surprise a year later she learned that one of her teachers had somehow gained access to her records and proceeded to tell other teachers that Karla was a homosexual. Before the year was over students were also beginning to tease both Karla and Pam about their relationship, pointing to them on the schoolground and calling them queer. It was at this point that she began to withdraw in earnest from contact with other students, spending more and more time with Pam.

When a neighbor informed her mother of the rumors going around about Karla she was called in for a joint conference with her father and mother which lasted most of the night. After much shouting, crying, threatening and pleading, Karla's mother forbade her to see Pam again. Taking away all of her shirts and blue jeans, her mother insisted that Karla wear nothing but dresses to school. She also insisted that she date boys and begin to prepare herself for marriage and a family. Too embarrassed to discuss with anyone her daughter's perverted behavior, as she called it, she also refused to consider psychiatric help for Karla when such was suggested by her husband.

Honoring her parents' wishes for several weeks, Karla soon began to see Pam in secret. Indicating to Mr. West once again that she was not really that interested in sex, although she had engaged in some sexual exploration together with Pam, Karla did admit that she loved females and had no desire to date males. Furthermore, she insisted that she had no desire to change as she was very happy with Pam. Her major problem was lack of acceptance by her parents and peers. At times she said that she became so angry that she wanted to kill people when they made remarks about her relationship with Pam. Her primary desire was to be left alone to live her life as she chose.

When Karla's mother learned that she had been seeing Pam behind her back she began to insist that Karla give an account of every minute of her time. Not permitted to leave the house unless accompanied by a family member, Karla had soon exploded and retaliated by telling her mother that she was gay, always had been and always would be. It was at this time that her mother decided to bring her to the mental health clinic, admitting for the first time that Karla was beyond her help.

Discussion

As with most parents upon learning that their child may be homosexual, Karla's parents reacted in a fashion which could only make a bad situation worse. The last thing that a child needs at a time like this is more rejection, especially from significant figures in their lives. No matter how angry or hurt parents may be that their child is homosexual, it is important that they communicate love and acceptance of the child even when they strongly disapprove of the behavior. Homosexuality is never cured by threats, yelling or sermons.

As for the prognosis in Karla's case, any hope for change would be minimized by her seemingly strong commitment to her current sexual life-style. When the desire to change is lacking, both the child and parents may profit from counseling. Regardless of Karla's expressed desire to continue her involvement with Pam, love and acceptance from her parents could go a long way in helping her confront the many problems she will encounter both personally and socially in the years ahead. If parents find it difficult to accept such a choice on the part of their child (and most parents would and understandably so), then counseling for the parents may be essential even when the child refuses to go herself.

Artie

Artie scheduled an appointment with the school counselor, Ms. Arnold, after his physical education teacher had heard him talking incoherently, cursing and banging on his gym locker the day before. When he had been unable to remember the combination to his lock he had ripped the upper part of the door from its hinges.

Described as a good student by his teachers, a quiet person who seemed to get along well with others, Artie appeared to be nervous and agitated in the initial visit with Ms. Arnold. In the session Artie focused primarily on a pain in his side which he described as severe and constant. Nervous and restless, he said he could no longer tolerate the pain and that something had to be done.

In exploring the matter further, Artie revealed that the pain became much worse when he was with other people. For this reason he stated that he avoided people whenever possible. Indicating that he hated any kind of discord, he would do anything to avoid a conflict and to keep peace.

Since his parents had never permitted Artie or his sister to fuss or raise their voices in the home, he said that he had learned the best way to get along and to avoid conflict was to keep quiet. Therefore, whenever any disagreement or conflict arose in his relationships with others he would leave rather than risk a confrontation. If he found himself unable to escape in this fashion, he would give in and do whatever was requested or demanded of him even when he did not want to.

Refusing to discuss in greater detail his personal feelings, Artie returned again and again in the session to ask if something could be done for the pain in his side. He said that he could put up with the rest if he could just get some relief from the pain. Asking if medication would help, he said that he would even be willing to undergo an operation if necessary. He continued to insist that his personal problems would be solved if he could just get rid of the pain.

Revealing that he had been to doctors, chiropractors, neurologists and had even asked for acupuncture, he complained that for some reason no one seemed able to alleviate his pain. Several physicians had suggested psychiatric help which he took as an insult and proof of their incompetence. In desperation he had agreed to schedule the appointment with his school counselor.

In the third session, still continuing to focus on his physical problems, Artie indicated that in recent weeks he had also begun to experience difficulty in going to sleep. Often when he would be near sleep or just waking up he would experience a strange feeling which he likened to sticking his finger in an open electric socket. He reported that he felt paralyzed from the waist up and found himself unable to move or to think clearly for about fifteen seconds. He sometimes felt as if some outside force was trying to possess his body and often felt that someone's spirit was in the room with him. These attacks were now occurring with such frequency that he dreaded going to bed.

Usually anxious and afraid during the sessions, he appeared at times to be near panic with a look of sheer terror crossing his face. At other times he would become so agitated that he would get up and walk around the room while talking with Ms. Arnold. At other times he would go off on tangents, having no relevance to what he was discussing at the moment. He confessed that he had a great fear of going crazy or losing control of himself as his mother had some years earlier. Except for this passing revelation he would not discuss her further.

After four sessions he gingerly expressed disappointment in the sessions, again indicating that he was not receiving any help with his main problem—namely his pain. Although he agreed to another appointment he failed to show up as scheduled.

Discussion

In many cases emotional problems are expressed in physical ways. Most of us on occasion have suffered from headaches due to emotional upset or tension. The digestive tract seems to be particularly sensitive to emotional turmoil or frustration. However, in cases such as this one, it appears that the physical symptoms are only a manifestation of a more serious problem which is primarily emotional. This is not to say that Artie's pains are nonexistent except in his mind. No matter the origin, the pain can be just as severe and authentic as if he were suffering from some major physical disorder. It is to say, however, that permanent relief will come only if and when the emotional components of his problems are recognized and dealt with. Once again, however, the responsibility for separating organically-derived from psychologically derived physical complaints should be left to the physician.

While many individuals manage with benefit of mental health aid to live with a host of physical symptoms for which no organic cause can be found, in Artie's case the severity of his problems justify referral for psychological help even though he opposes this kind of help.

There are also other clues which suggest that he needs psychological help—his uncontrollable outbursts as evidenced by his attack on his locker, his fear of and difficulty in sleeping, and his bizarre and unrealistic experiences and thoughts as described in the episodes in which he feels that he is being possessed by spirits. Additional concern arises from his inability to deal with stress or to form relationships with people. Finally, his homelife, including the restrictions against the expression of normal feelings and his mother's emotional history all suggest the need for further exploration.

In summary psychological help may be needed if the child or student

1. Continues to insist there is something seriously wrong physically when there is no organic reason to suspect that such is true. Individuals have been known in more serious cases to focus on some minor physical impairment or imperfection to the point that they become so obsessed with the matter that they can no longer function.

2. Sees, hears, tastes, feels or smells things which are not there.

3. Frequently experiences feelings of terror, fear or panic without sufficient cause.

4. Is incoherent or behaves in an irrational or bizarre fashion.

5. Feels that he is being possessed, controlled or manipulated by some strange or unseen force outside himself.

6. Is unduly distrustful, irritable or angry.

7. Withdraws or isolates himself and is unable to relate to or form meaningful relationships with peers, teachers and family.

8. Appears unable to express appropriate feelings or emotions.

9. Engages in behavior which is grossly inappropriate for the specific situation.

10. Is unduly anxious, depressed or tense frequently and/or for long periods of time.

11. Shows evidence of a drastic or sudden change in personality or way of functioning.

Mitzi

Mitzi's mother had brought Mitzi to Dr. Moore's office after Mitzi had taken ten aspirin. Mitzi stated that she had done so because she could no longer cope with her feelings of despair. As she talked Mitzi was interrupted by her mother who confessed that she no longer knew how to approach her daughter. It was learned from Mitzi and her mother that Mitzi, a fifteen-year-old sophomore, had for the last six months experienced swings in mood to the point that neither she nor her parents could predict how she would respond to any given situation. Even her teachers and friends had told her that she was so unpredictable that they never knew how to relate to her or what to expect. Both Mitzi and her mother agreed that she might wake up one morning in a great mood followed the next day by a mood so foul or depressed that even her parents and her sister stayed away from her.

At times she was so anxious that she could not go to sleep. At other times she did nothing but sleep. Indicating that she felt as if she always had an umbrella over her head, getting lower and lower, she had given up many of the activities both at school and church which she had enjoyed.

Further questioning revealed that Mitzi had recently begun to lose her hair. In searching for the causes it was learned that for reasons unknown to her, Mitzi would pluck hairs from her head while studying or talking with friends. Not immediately obvious because of her long hair, close examination revealed two bald spots on the back side of her head.

Mitzi also complained of a desire to eat constantly, and though she was actually slender, she wanted to lose at least seven more pounds. Indeed, she said, this was a major concern and despite Dr. Moore's statement that she was already slightly underweight for her age and height, Mitzi continued to insist that she would look and feel better if she could lose the additional pounds. This was so important to her, she confessed, that she had been taking pills to suppress her appetite. Admitting that she had acquired them from a friend at school, she stated that she had been taking them for the last six months whenever she could get them. Despite her desire to lose weight she indicated that at times she had an uncontrollable urge to eat and sneaked candy and cookies into her room at night and ate until she was sick. Feeling bad after doing so, she would then get back on her pills and a rigid diet for several days.

Returning again to a discussion of her moodiness, Mitzi added that on certain days she felt very good. However, the following day, for no obvious reason, she could hardly muster the effort to get up out of her chair. She would sit immobilized for long periods of time in her chair. At such times even answering the phone was an unbearable chore. She later indicated that she spent a major portion of her time daydreaming. Mitzi admitted that she would become so immersed in her fantasies that her parents would have to call her several times before she heard. When her parents would chide her for such behavior she would reply that her dreaming was the only thing which made her existence possible in a world she found so intolerable.

At other times she would feel as if the words coming from her mouth belonged to someone else. Even while reciting in class she would sometimes feel as if she were back in her seat observing herself in front of the room talking. Describing such feelings as weird and strange she asked, "Does this mean I am crazy?"

Reassuring Mitzi that she was certainly not crazy, Dr. Moore, with Mitzi's and her mother's permission, arranged an appointment for further evaluation.

Discussion

Even though Dr. Moore assured Mitzi that she was not crazy, whatever that may mean, Mitzi was obviously experiencing problems which called for psychological attention. Of major concern was her attempt to harm herself. At best her attempt to harm herself was a rather far-out and desperate way of asking for help and attention. Such is in itself a definite indication of the need for psychological intervention. At its worst it can be fatal.

There are those who would imply that if she had really been

intent on killing herself Mitzi would have taken more than ten aspirin tablets. They might then suggest that Mitzi was only seeking attention. However, it should be stressed in working with adolescents and children, who are less sophisticated in their knowledge of drugs than adults, that children sometimes fail in their efforts to kill themselves simply because they misjudge the dosage necessary to do the job. In such cases the size or number of pills swallowed is a poor indicator or predictor of their true intent. No matter the basic intent, psychological evaluation is imperative.

Regarding Mitzi's depression and daydreaming it should be said that all people get depressed and that all people daydream, either for sheer enjoyment or to escape the pressures of life. While adults get depressed more than children and children daydream more than adults, the fact remains that both children and adults share in such experiences from time to time. However, in this case, degree is the crucial measure.

Both Mitzi's depression and her daydreaming seem to be out of proportion with the average, normal-type, transient depression. The depth of her depression might be gauged by her suicide attempt.

Depression may, in many cases, be traced to an event or situation which has occurred in the life of the depressed person. This can involve the loss of a loved one through death or separation, failure in school or some other meaningful endeavor, or for a thousand other reasons. Under such conditions, grief and depression, while painful, are understandable, even healthy. Depression due to such causes is usually easier to treat.

Depression which cannot be linked to any definite or reasonable cause is more difficult to diagnose and treat. While there are medications which can be used to treat such depression, authorities are not certain as to the causes. Whatever the cause of depression, it should never be permitted to continue for any long period of time without professional evaluation.

Mitzi's daydreaming is also excessive to the point that it is seriously interfering with her school work and her interaction with her family. By her own admission, fantasizing has been selected as the chief outlet from a world she finds intolerable.

Her frequent and drastic changes in mood are further causes for concern. Her obsession with her weight, even when she is already underweight, along with her loss of hair are still other ways in which emotionally disturbed individuals signal in physical ways that they are experiencing underlying mental and emotional problems.

Her feelings of depersonalization are another way in which emotionally disturbed individuals often see themselves as detached or distant from themselves and reality. Her erratic sleeping and eating habits, which may tend toward excess in both directions, too much or too little, are also good indicators that the individual may be experiencing emotional difficulties.

While there are many and varied symptoms which may be displayed by the depressed person, depression should be considered and help sought if the child or student

1. Experiences for any length of time difficulty in eating or sleeping. This can include difficulty in going to sleep, waking up often during the night or early morning awakening. Wanting to sleep most of the time to the exclusion of other activities or interests is another possible indicator that something is wrong. Eating habits may be affected to the point that the child suffers a severe loss of appetite or wants to eat all the time. Once physical causes are ruled out, depression is often the diagnosis.

2. Experiences a loss of sexual desire or interest in the opposite sex. This is of course more applicable to the older and more sexually-developed individual.

3. Suffers from a general loss of interest in life, school, work, relationships, play, hobbies, etc.

4. Withdraws from human contact or has excessive need for solitude.

5. Experiences great sadness or cries often for no apparent reason.

6. Has low self-esteem or feelings of worthlessness.

7. Is unreasonably dissatisfied with physical appearance, as in the matter of Mitzi's weight.

8. Experiences strong feelings of helplessness or hopelessness.
9. Shows signs of lethargy or lack of concern for personal appearance or personal habits. This is particularly true if previously the child has taken great interest or pride in such matters.
10. Shows other signs of mental disturbance.
11. Resorts to over-the-counter diet suppressants or street-purchased speed which have a temporary mood-elevating effect.

Despite the popularity of appetite-suppressing drugs as an easy way to lose weight, the results have been disappointing. Even under medical supervision there may be dangerous side effects. As a result physicians recommend such medication only in certain medical situations. It cannot be emphasized too strongly that such medication should never be taken without medical supervision.

Duke

Duke, an eighteen-year-old senior, came to see Mr. Bick, the school counselor, complaining that he could no longer concentrate on his studies. Previously a very good student with an active social life, he had in the last year begun to withdraw more and more. Spending most of his time in his room watching television, he had not dated in six months. However, even television failed to hold his attention for any length of time because of the many thoughts which kept creeping into his head. He said that at times it seemed as if he were being bombarded by a thousand thoughts at one time. Admitting that they were trivial things, he nonetheless could not push them from his mind.

Describing his activities in more detail, he indicated that while watching television he would become so concerned about his clothes that he would get up and unpack his drawers, counting his shirts and socks several times to make sure that they matched. At other times, determined not to give in to such an urge, he would try to study, only to end up sitting, sometimes for two or three hours, thinking about the particular urge rather than concentrating on his work.

At times he would succumb to the urge to clean out his closet and would give away most of his clothes. The next day he could not rest until he had purchased new clothes. After doing so he usually felt guilty for spending the money. A great lover of house plants, he insisted that all plants be in pots of the same color. If he purchased one in a different-colored pot he felt ill at ease until he had repainted the pot.

Although he masturbated daily, he said that he did not do so because of any strong sexual feelings but because it was something to do. He denied ever having had any sexual relationships with anyone. He had wondered on occasion if he might not have homosexual inclinations. He sometimes became so preoccupied with this concern at night that he was unable to go to sleep. Even though he was pretty sure that he was not homosexual he said that he stayed away from males as much as possible just to be on the safe side. He had also begun to smoke pot seven months earlier and now smoked almost every night alone in his room.

Even though his parents insisted that he get out more and become involved socially, he stated that he preferred to be alone. Admitting that he knew it was bad to isolate himself so much, he expressed a fear of becoming involved with anyone.

When asked about his frequent use of pot by Mr. Bick, Duke responded that it was the only thing which helped him to relax and forget his problems. Confessing that he had tried other drugs including downers, LSD and speed, he had become frightened after a bad trip on LSD and now used pot exclusively.

Discussion

There are several disturbing factors in Duke's case which suggest a need for psychological assistance. These include his inability to concentrate or relax and his compelling need to perform tasks over and over again even when he admits they are trivial. His obsessive concern about being homosexual and his need to masturbate daily even when he felt no urge to do so are also reason for concern. While most authorities agree that masturbation is usually a normal and healthy function of adolescence, in

Duke's case it seemed to be a substitute for human involvement and a further indication that he was adopting more and more a pattern of withdrawal and doing things alone.

As for drugs it should be emphasized that as with alcohol, most people who smoke pot are not mentally ill. A large percentage of young people experiment with pot and alcohol with no obvious ill effects. Others resort to the use of barbiturates, hallucinogens or amphetamines, some with no immediately visible bad results. Though there is abundant speculation without any widely accepted explanation, a significant number of individuals have engaged in the use of drugs with severe emotional consequences. Whether such individuals turn to drugs because they are already experiencing emotional problems or whether they become emotionally disturbed after usage is often difficult to determine. While there is much that we do not know about certain drugs we do know that use or misuse of many drugs can be harmful, even fatal. With others, including marijuana, there are still many questions to be answered despite the many arguments on both sides being presented at the present.

We do know that drugs are a serious problem in this country for both children and adults. This includes those already on the borderline emotionally and the so-called normal adolescent wishing to try something new. An increasingly recognized process of drug abuse involves the youngster or adult who repeatedly obtains medicine prescribed by their physician. While many parents are concerned about the use of certain drugs by their children, and justifiably so, we should be reminded that alcohol is still by far the number one drug problem in this country.

Since most individuals are exposed to a wide range of materials and information concerning the dangers of drugs it hardly seems necessary to reproduce here the information disseminated daily on television and in various publications.

Suffice it to say, in Duke's case, his heavy use of marijuana as his only means to relax is obviously a danger signal. While he will never become addicted to pot as medically defined, his psychological dependence on the drug combined with his compulsive and obsessive behavior as described above indicates a definite need for psychological referral. He has become dysfunctional both socially and academically. Without psychological referral only withdrawal can help him avoid situations that will arouse further compulsive behavior. Additionally, his only means to quell his obsessive thinking, which is obviously very anxiety provoking, is to seek the temporary solace that pot brings him.

Alan

Alan, an eighteen-year-old senior and member of the school basketball team, entered Coach Russell's office shortly after practice one afternoon to inform him that he was quitting the team. One of the steadiest, if not the most gifted athlete on the team, Alan had been counted on for the coming year to play a major role in the team's efforts to better their previous year's record. Priding himself on being close to his players, it was only after considerable effort that Coach Russell was able to draw from Alan his reasons for quitting. Although he had noticed that Alan had been especially jumpy since practice began, he had attributed it to the excitement of a new season and was surprised to hear Alan say that he was quitting because he could no longer tolerate the idea of drinking from the same water fountain or using the same restroom and showers used by the rest of the team. Extracting a promise from Alan that he would not leave the team until he had talked with the school psychologist, Coach Russell arranged an appointment for Alan the following day.

In the first session, it was learned that Alan's fear of germs had been present for several years but had gotten worse in his senior year. It had become so bad that he no longer ate in the school cafeteria. He brought his own lunch from home in an airtight container which he washed in boiling water for fifteen minutes each day. At home, if visitors came to eat, he would insist that their dishes be washed when they left and placed in boiling water for fifteen minutes. His fear of germs and dirt also prompted him to wash his own hands each time he touched a door knob or handled a piece of money. At times he would wash his hands until they were raw and chapped. No matter how much he suffered he would never use a restroom on a trip or at school.

Even though he could recognize and admit that his fears were unfounded and his behavior extreme, Alan insisted that he could not keep from behaving as he did. Even when he sat down and tried to study he often found himself unable to concentrate on his studies and to keep his mind off germs. When he tried to push such thoughts from his mind and failed, he would get up and start cleaning his room or washing his hands or dishes for a second or third time. As a result of the time spent in such activities he was falling behind in his school work.

Discussion

Most young children develop irrational or unfounded fears. Even adults who are otherwise considered to be normal by their friends often develop similar fears in which, for reasons unknown to them, they shy away from or avoid completely specific objects, places or situations. Most of us know someone who is afraid to ride an elevator or afraid of high places. Most children outgrow these fears. Many adults continue to function quite well despite certain mild phobias by avoiding the situation which causes them anxiety.

In some cases, however, as with Alan, the anxiety and fear become so great or widespread that they grossly interfere with the person's ability to function or to perform daily tasks. In more serious cases individuals may become so anxious and terrified that they are almost totally incapacitated. The objects or situations around which the fear may be focused are without limit. It may involve fear of open places, animals, germs, crowds, airplanes or a host of other situations as well as animate or inanimate objects. Two of the more common phobias have to do with fear of closed places and heights.

Individuals thus affected seldom respond to attempts by well-meaning persons to rid them of their fears through logic, reason or assurances that they will be safe. It is believed that most of these irrational fears are the result of attempts by the individual to deal with some internal anxiety or emotion which he is unable to face consciously. As a result he may unconsciously select some specific object onto which he can displace his anxieties. The feeling is now external and can be avoided.

When individuals choose to live with minor phobias rather than undergo therapy, there is little that can be done in the way of suggesting help. While such ongoing irrational fears and anxieties are much more significant in older children and adults than in small children, they should not be ignored in either case. Parents and teachers should be concerned and suggest that children talk with the school counselor, psychologist or other mental health professional if the child

1. Seems unusually fearful or anxious about any particular object or situation. While it is normal, for example, to have some fear of high places since they can pose a potential threat to safety, an extreme fear suggests that more than just a normal reaction to high places may be present.

2. Obviously avoids going to the restroom, drinking from school water fountains, etc.

3. Is unusually meticulous and concerned about germs, dirt or cleanliness.

4. Washes hands excessively or performs any other ritual regularly.

5. Becomes physically ill, feels faint or unduly anxious in specific situations.

6. Behaves as if compelled to do something even when reason dictates otherwise.

These are just a few of the many ways in which phobias may be manifested. As in evaluating the potential for emotional disturbance in all situations, one of the most significant indicators is that of appropriateness. In any situation in which individuals respond in such a way as to be considered grossly inappropriate for their particular age group there is reason to suggest a conference with parents or referral to the school counselor for further evaluation.

Celia

Celia, recently elected homecoming queen in her high school, came to see Ms. Mays, the school psychologist, with the complaint that she felt empty and unhappy. Blessed with a beautiful face and a lovely figure, Celia had also been a cheerleader for three years and had been selected the best-looking girl in the eleventh grade the previous year.

In discussing her family, Celia described her father as a self-made man, very successful in business, who had provided his family with anything money could buy. Although they were not a close family, Celia indicated that her home life was a comfortable one and that she had no complaints about her childhood.

Speculating about the causes for her unhappiness Celia ventured the opinion that her upcoming graduation might be part of the problem. She had become so accustomed to being the center of attention that the thought of no longer being in the spotlight after graduation disturbed her. Although she intended to go to college, she was afraid that she might not be able to compete with the other girls there for cheerleader or in the other areas she had been so active in as a high school student.

Very popular with boys, who viewed her as sexy and provocative, Celia dated a large number of different boys. However, her dates, interpreting her come-on looks and behaviors as an invitation to sex, were shocked when they tried to park or even kiss her goodnight. When her dates accused her of being a cold fish, complaining of the inconsistency between her flirtatious attitude and her conduct on dates, Celia insisted that she did not know what they were talking about.

Admitting that many guys did make passes at her, Celia stated that she could not understand why they did since she never encouraged such a response. Confessing that she did place a great premium on looking nice, she liked to wear tight pants, shorts or low-cut blouses whenever the circumstances permitted. While indicating that she enjoyed the looks and attention, she added that this did not mean that she was on the make for every boy in school and really hated them pawing her on dates.

A nervous and easily excited person, Celia said she became depressed when not involved in something. She cried easily but also seemed to bubble over with enthusiasm at other times. She especially liked social get-togethers and was usually considered great fun at parties. Expressing no difficulty in those situations where large numbers of people were involved, her major problems occurred when she was alone or involved in a one-to-one relationship. She did not enjoy deep discussions or talk of problems. She preferred to have fun and enjoy life.

In class she had never been a good student, but managed to get by on her charm and good looks. Not only was she unwittingly coy and seductive toward male classmates, she displayed the same behavior towards her male teachers. Much to her horror, one of the younger coaches had recently suggested a date. Surprised that he would even think that she would consider dating a teacher, Celia admitted that she had somehow found herself going by his office daily on her way to cheerleaders' practice. Even though she had no classes with him she managed to find reasons to stop by and chat awhile each day.

Discussion

It is frequently difficult for teachers or parents to understand or take seriously the complaints of young girls like Celia. They do so for the reason that many such complaints come from young women who seem to have everything. They are often beautiful and talented. They may be cheerleaders or beauty contestants. They are frequently very popular and hold many student offices. They could be described as jet set teenagers, the envy of their classmates.

Despite their many attributes and successes, many of these young people complain of emptiness, unhappiness and a lack of meaning in their lives. These individuals have an almost insatiable need for attention and seem unhappy when not in the limelight. They are often very superficial in their thinking and immature. While they may seem to be the life of the party, they often have difficulty in the more serious business of day-to-day living. In more intimate personal relationships they may appear very uncomfortable.

Although sexually seductive, they usually do not engage in such behavior for sexual reasons, but for attention. Males, both young and old, responding to their coyness as some sort of sexual overture are in for a big surprise. In more serious cases such young females may cry "rape" or complain to their parents that some boy or man is making sexual advances which they find frightening or disgusting. They never seem to see any correlation between their girlish seductiveness and the response they receive from males. Many will deny that they do anything to arouse sexual interest but are simply being taken advantage of by some sex-crazy man or boy.

Like Celia, such females can be both highly excitable and exciting. While often very friendly, with a smile and cheery greeting for everyone, they often do so in order to be popular or gain the approval they so desperately crave rather than from any sincere concern for others.

It is important that these individuals receive psychological help at an early age. Inner strengths and resources need to be developed lest at a later time they may become desperate when their physical attractiveness begins to wane or they are forced to retire from the public eye due to graduation, motherhood or some other less glamorous undertaking. Failure to adjust or accept themselves when life situations change may result in the insecure teenage girl turning into a younger version of the insecure adult female who attempts to prove that she is still attractive and desirable by attempting to seduce her minister, lawyer or doctor under the pretense of seeking the professional services they have to offer. As the bloom of youth fades and the chances of ego-sustaining feedback diminish, the growth insecurity can become the pathway to a long-term depression.

Lola

At the request of Lola's teachers a meeting had been arranged with the principal to discuss Lola's frequent and unprovoked confrontations with her teachers. In the ensuing discussion it was learned that Lola, a sixteen-year-old junior, had been a source of trouble since she entered the school two years earlier. She had experienced difficulty with every one of her teachers at one time or another. Not only did she have problems with the teachers but with other students as well. Due to her temper and caustic personality most of the other students were afraid of her.

During the meeting each teacher described Lola as a person who took offense very easily. At the slightest hint of criticism she would turn red in the face and then explode verbally. She had slapped several classmates and cursed teachers as well. Most teachers, realizing that Lola did get angry easily, went out of their way to be nice and made a sincere effort to win her over. At times things would go along well for several days with various teachers feeling they had made progress in working with Lola. Suddenly, and for some small reason, Lola would erupt.

Several of her teachers indicated that Lola seemed to go out of her way to create dissension in the classroom. As if looking for a run-in with teachers, she would deliberately disobey and openly flaunt her disregard for their position. She laughed and talked with other students at will in class despite teachers' requests that she not do so. If called down she would become argumentative and on several occasions had walked out of class to call her mother or complain to the principal that she was being mistreated. At other times she would barge into a class in the middle of a lecture, deliberately creating noise and disrupting the entire class. If her teachers tried to ignore her, she would continue to smirk or bait them until, in frustration, they would send her to the principal's office.

In almost every case when this happened Lola would then go home and tell her mother, in an exaggerated fashion, how she had been mistreated. The mother would immediately get on the phone or come to the principal's office demanding that something be done about the treatment of her daughter. On numerous occasions after thinking that things had been resolved to the mother's satisfaction and both mother and daughter had been placated, the principal would receive a call at night from the school superintendent indicating that he had just received a complaint from Lola's mother about the situation. If Lola's mother did not receive satisfaction from either she had on occasion called school board members and cursed them.

Discussion

Children at all ages need recognition and attention. They will usually get it in some way or other or else suffer severe consequences. The child who is constantly misbehaving or showing off in class is probably seeking to meet the same need as the child who becomes a successful actor in the school play. Fortunately most children seek attention in constructive ways. They may seek to achieve recognition by being good students, cheerleaders football players, running for student office or in a number of other socially acceptable ways.

Unfortunately, Lola chose to seek attention in ways which were both destructive and disrupting. The bedlam and chaos created by Lola in her attempts to get attention worked without question, however the methods used to gain attention created problems not only for Lola but for other students, teachers and administrators as well.

It is also interesting that Lola always went to her mother with her complaints. This, along with her tendency to stretch the truth to make the situation worse than it really was, suggests that Lola was not getting the need for recognition satisfied within her immediate family. If Lola believed that she could get her mother's attention only if she went to such extremes, this could explain her need to behave in such a fashion. The mother's response only served to reinforce Lola's behavior and to convince her that she could be assured of continuing to get attention with such extreme behavior. Whatever her reasons for acting as she did, both mother and daughter need help, and efforts should be made to refer both for counseling.

In those cases in which parents discover that their child is being victimized by some teacher unjustly they should take immediate steps to remedy the situation by talking with the teacher or school officials. If this fails and the situation persists after all reasonable alternatives have been exhausted, parents can many times help the child realize that life demands that we sometimes adjust to situations which are not to our liking. In concept, justice is a highly desirable principle and one for which we should always struggle. However justice and right do not always prevail. While it is one of the most frustrating lessons we have to learn as human beings, it is also one of the most important. Helping children and students learn to cope with the many injustices which life thrusts upon them is one of the most significant tasks of both home and school.

Parents and teachers, like all human beings, are not always fair in their relationships with children. In those situations in which the child is being treated unjustly by some teacher (or other situation in life) parents need to listen and provide support and nurturance. This does not mean that parents should immediately jump to attack the teacher. As we know only too well, far too many parents and children already blame teachers for everything that happens to the child. One of the greatest mistakes a parent can make is to side with the child against the teacher in every instance in which problems arise in the school without first investigating the situation thoroughly.

This seems to have been the case with Lola and her mother. If they are unwilling to seek psychological help it is very probable that both Lola and her mother will continue to be very unhappy individuals as well as create havoc and distress for those around them.

Chapter 5

CHECKLIST OF SYMPTOMS

IN THE PRECEDING PAGES we have centered, in large measure, on the early detection of the emotionally disturbed child and adolescent by teachers and parents. We have emphasized the need for early recognition and treatment because the chances for change and improvement are significantly greater if treatment is initiated during these critical years in which children and adolescents are establishing patterns of relating to their world which will, in many cases, endure for a lifetime.

In an attempt to provide assistance to parents and teachers interested in learning more about the emotionally disturbed child we have relied heavily on the use of case studies and discussion. In an effort to present in summary fashion some of the information contained in earlier chapters we have prepared a list of symptoms which can be used by parents and teachers in identifying the child with possible emotional problems. We have included within this body of symptoms some of the danger signals most often transmitted whenever mental illness is present.

The reader is again cautioned that any one or combination of the symptoms listed below does not necessarily mean that the child is mentally ill. They are also reminded that behavior displayed at one age may be very appropriate, but inappropriate if seen at a later age. For example, bed wetting or fear of the dark in a child of three are quite a different matter than in a child of seven.

We should also be reminded that mental illness is in large part socially defined. There are no hard and fast rules. What is defined as normal behavior in one culture may be seen as grossly abnormal in another culture. The child living in an upper middle-class neighborhood who is frequently fighting or stealing food and money is, in all probability, experiencing psychological problems serious enough to warrant psychiatric help. On the other hand, the

138

child reared in some ghetto where violence and poverty are a way of life may be stealing and fighting just to stay alive. While this is not good, it does not necessarily mean that the child is mentally ill.

Despite the difficulty in defining mental illness there are certain danger signals which suggest the need for further evaluation. If the child or adolescent displays any of the following symptoms, parents and teachers should be alert to the possibility of emotional problems and seek psychological evaluation.

Symptoms

Birth to Six Months:
constant crying
absence of crying
lack of responsiveness
overactivity/no activity
no smiling
no grasping
no visual focusing on objects

Six to Twelve Months:
no sitting up
inability to recognize mother's face
no manipulation of body parts
no playing with toys
no attempts at crawling, sitting up or walking
severe or prolonged problems eating or sleeping
(should be investigated at any age.)

One to Two Years:
frequent nightmares
excessive fear of strangers
lack of curiosity
no exploration
excessive fear of darkness
no/little verbalization
unduly quiet

Two to Four Years:
clinging to mother
fear of father
intolerance to change

head banging
serious delay or difficulties in toi-
    let training
violent or destructive
excessive temper tantrums
prefers being alone to being with
    other children
fear of separation

Four to Six Years: invisible friend
no fantasy life acted out
no imitation of parental activities
fear of school
low level of energy
frequent stomachaches, headaches,
    vomiting
inability to move body parts
absence of sexual exploration of
    self and peers
slow learner
frequent fights
excessively obedient
excessively neat
nail biting
pulling out hair
hallucinations
total absence of temper outbursts

First through Twelfth Grades: withdrawal from social relationships
cannot tolerate closeness or affec-
    tion
cannot get along with peers
resistance to all authority
unusually irritable and quarrelsome
fights a lot, bullying and abusive
    toward others
gets angry easily and often
frequent temper tantrums, violent
    outbursts, etc.

likes to hurt others, brutal, cruel, punitive

likes to hurt animals

enjoys violence

destructive of property

stealing, lying or cheating often

exploitation of others

lack of conscience or feelings of guilt or remorse when caught doing something wrong

too passive and quiet

too good

perfectionistic

never expresses ideas or opinions

never shows feelings (anger, love, warmth, etc.)

overly shy, timid or inhibited

excessive daydreaming or other forms of escape (television, movies, studies, books, work, etc.)

inflicts punishment on self, either physically or mentally

encourages punishment of self by others

prolonged periods of elation without sufficient reason

unduly depressed frequently

unduly anxious frequently

sets impossible standards for self and others

overly concerned with neatness and order

constant worrier

ritualistic behavior, excessive hand-washing, not stepping on cracks, etc.

feeling that one is compelled to do something over and over when reason and pleasure dictate otherwise

low self-esteem

lacking in self-control

feelings of helplessness and hope-lessness

feelings of being controlled by others or some mysterious force

overreacts (cries easily or gets angry over little things)

thinking or talking of suicide (or more subtle indications of in-tent)

inability to relax and have fun

overly strict conscience or strong sense of guilt

drastic changes in personal habits

self-neglect or lack of concern for personal appearance

rapid change in moods or person-ality

nervous, fidgety, inattentive and disruptive in class or home

thumbsucking

bedwetting

tics

stuttering or other speech difficul-ties

difficulty in learning to read, write or talk

other learning disorders

lack of ability to solve problems usually handled with ease by age group

mental confusion

delusions (false beliefs even when circumstances or common sense dictate otherwise; may include such things as believing that one is God, that someone is trying to harm them, etc.)

hallucinations (false sensory perceptions which may involve such things as seeing or hearing nonexistent voices or things)

unduly suspicious or distrustful

overly sensitive to criticism

feelings that things about one's self or environment are not real

feelings of being detached from one's self or body

frequent physical complaints for which no organic cause can be found

frequent or severe headaches or stomachaches

noticeably overweight or underweight

eating problems (loss of appetite, desire to eat constantly, refusal to eat, etc.)

sleep disturbance (can't sleep, desire to sleep all the time, nightmares, waking up often, etc.)

loss of interest and enthusiasm in general

chronic fatigue and loss of energy

loss of consciousness, blackouts or dream-like states in which child seems unaware of what is going on around him.

visual problems (blurred or double vision, unable to focus or co-ordinate eyes)

convulsions or seizures

clumsiness, lack of physical coordi-nation, frequent stumbling, falling, jerking movements, etc.

loss of memory, forgetfulness

great concern with witchcraft, demons, etc.

drug abuse (including alcohol)

no sexual curiosity or interest

sexual promiscuity

homosexuality (see cases for discus-sion of normal and abnormal behavior between members of same sex)

incest

undue concern about other sexual matters

inappropriate behavior (laughing when crying seems called for, ignoring the death of a parent or sibling as if nothing had happened, etc.)

excessive or senseless giggling, cry-ing, gesturing, gibberish, etc.

accident-proneness or undue risk-taking behavior

any exaggerated or irrational fear (This may include fear of eleva-tors, the dark, high places, going to school, death and many more.)

excessive feelings of loneliness and alienation

deterioration of mental perform-ance

lack of physical and mental development in keeping with age
group
overly dependent
highly excitable
immaturity or inability to postpone gratification

In addition to the symptoms listed above there are other situations in which youngsters are apt to experience varying degrees of
psychological trauma and should be watched. For example, the
child who is a victim of child abuse is a good candidate to develop emotional problems if they are not already present. Parents
and teachers should also be alert to the need for help on the part
of children who have recently lost a parent due to death, divorce
or abandonment. Children from deprived homes, especially those
in which love and affection are withheld, form still another likely
group of candidates for emotional problems. Children from homes
with a family history of mental illness also tend to need special
attention as do those from families in which either parent may
have a serious drug or drinking problem.

One final note—In attempting to determine if a child is experiencing emotional problems, two key words should be mentioned—*appropriate* and *extreme*. Most children manifest some of
the symptoms listed above at various times in their lives. In most
cases they are no cause for major concern. However, if parents and
teachers are in doubt about a particular child's behavior, they
might ask themselves two questions—(1) Is the behavior extreme? (2)
Is it grossly inappropriate? If the answer to either of these questions is yes, then the child may be in need of further evaluation.

Chapter 6

WHERE CAN PARENTS AND TEACHERS GO FOR HELP?

ONCE IT IS SUSPECTED that the child or adolescent is in need of psychological help, the question arises, "Where does the parent or teacher turn for help?" In this chapter we would like to mention some of the resources available in most communities for the treatment of the emotionally disturbed.

Contrary to what many believe, there are many individuals in addition to psychiatrists who are qualified to provide psychological assistance. These may include psychologists, physicians, social workers, guidance counselors, clergymen and marriage and family counselors.

Referral Sources

A. *Schools.* Within the school itself there are a number of specialists qualified to work with various types of emotional problems. These may include school psychologists, guidance counselors, speech therapists, teachers for the emotionally disturbed or mentally retarded, specialists in reading and other teachers trained to work with students experiencing behavioral or learning disorders. In many school systems a psychiatrist may be available on a part-time consulting basis.

These professionals may offer a variety of services including vocational counseling, testing, individual counseling, group therapy, sensitivity training, growth or human development training, or help in learning to read or overcome some behavioral or learning disorders.

B. *Community.* One of the quickest ways to obtain information about referral sources is to contact the local or nearby community mental health center. Since 1964, under the Mental Health Acts, a network of such centers has evolved throughout the country. One center may cover one county or ten. The territory it

services is known as its catchment area. To obtain help all it takes
is usually a phone call if you live within the catchment area. Such
centers offer a number of services and may include such professionals as psychiatrists, psychologists, family counselors, psychiatric
social workers and psychiatric nurses. Most have access to a nearby
hospital equipped with psychiatric facilities for the treatment of
the more seriously emotionally disturbed.

In larger urban areas or at major universities there are usually
a variety of clinics specializing in the treatment of children. They
may be referred to as child guidance centers or may exist under a
variety of other titles. They are designed, however, to work especially with children experiencing problems.

Other agencies in the community working with children may
include family service agencies, welfare agencies or hospitals which
treat emotionally disturbed children on both an inpatient and
outpatient basis.

C. *Private.* In rural areas the number of mental health professionals in private practice may be limited or nonexistent. A
large percentage of psychiatrists, for example, are located in large
cities. However, there does seem to be a trend in which more psychiatrists and psychologists are setting up practices in smaller
towns and rural areas than was true even five years ago.

In urban areas the number of mental health professionals available to work with the emotionally troubled is unlimited. However, the number who specialize in working with children and
adolescents is significantly smaller and should be considered in
looking for help for children or adolescents. Many psychiatrists or
psychologists may be very effective in working with adults but
have limited experience in working with younger age groups. In
addition, there are various private clinics, agencies, hospitals and
other institutions that offer services to families and children for
a fee. There are also a number of schools throughout the country
which work exclusively with emotionally troubled children.

In most cases any child or adult needing psychiatric help can
now obtain such help quickly and efficiently. With the development in recent years of community mental health agencies and
regional hospitals this help can usually be found near home. This

is in sharp contrast to the past in which help for the emotionally troubled consisted primarily of confinement in a large state hospital. If hospitalization is required now it is usually possible to receive treatment in a much smaller and more up-to-date facility. With new medicines and methods of treatment the confinement rate has dropped considerably with most patients now being treated on an outpatient basis.

As for costs, most of the services provided in schools are free as part of the school program. Community mental health agencies usually have a sliding scale based on the ability to pay. If unable to pay, treatment is still provided. For those seeking the services of a mental health professional in private practice the cost is considerably higher.

In those cases in which parents and teachers are uncertain about the referral sources available in the community, such information can usually be obtained by calling the county medical society or the public health department. Some communities publish a booklet listing all the agencies and facilities available in the surrounding area.

In any discussion involving the referral of children for psychological or behavioral reasons we would be remiss if we chose to ignore the feelings of parents and teachers when treatment for mental illness becomes necessary for their child or student.

While it is important that parents and teachers be made aware of their roles and responsibilities regarding the emotional health of children, it is just as important that they not go overboard in doing so. Most parents, on first learning that their child is emotionally ill, experience strong feelings of guilt, self-recrimination, anger, frustration, and even marital conflict or some other painful emotion. Indeed, not only parents, but all protagonists inside the nuclear family containing the dysfunctional member, as well as teachers and others outside the family, usually suffer in their own way.

Whenever such a crisis arises one of the most common reactions is for the parents to see themselves as having failed as parents. Quite often, in an attempt to allay personal feelings of guilt and suffering, the mother may blame the father or vice versa.

Another version of blame placing is for one parent to ally herself or himself with the child and to blame the parents excluded from the alliance.

When the family finds itself visited by the misfortune of having a child or adolescent afflicted with some emotional and/or physiological disorder, it is important that family members not become bogged down in placing blame. Rather than blame placing the important thing is for the family to come together and attempt, with professional help, to find ways to help the troubled child as well as each other. In most cases, if this is done, something can be done which will promote more generally satisfying outcomes.

Whenever a child is found to be mentally ill, it is imperative that parents and teachers not be made to feel that the emotionally troubled child is a product of their badness. Unfortunately, some mental health professionals manage to create overwhelming feelings of guilt in parents when mental illness strikes the family. Cases have been known in which parents have endured long years of needless suffering because they had been told by some psychiatrist or psychologist that they were responsible for their child's illness. This is, in our opinion, most inappropriate. We just do not know enough about the causes of mental illness to make such a charge. Mental and emotional illness is the result of a multiplicity of causes rather than any one event or relationship gone awry. If there is to be blame, our lack of psychological knowledge is the more appropriate culprit.

Chapter 7

THE PROMOTION OF
GOOD MENTAL HEALTH

GOOD MENTAL HEALTH is no accident. As with physical fitness it is too important to be left entirely to chance. With this in mind we would like to discuss in this chapter some of the things we feel teachers and parents might do to promote the cause of better mental health in children and students during these most crucial years of childhood and adolescence.

While there are conditions, both mentally and physically, over which we seem to have little control, there are certain basic rules regarding the creation of an environment, both at home and at school, which would, in our opinion, increase significantly the chances of children and alolescents growing and developing into emotionally healthy individuals. A brief discussion of some of these requirements follows.

Awareness

The first prerequisite for the establishment of an atmosphere conducive to the development of good mental health in the home and school is an awareness on the part of parents and teachers of the influence they have on their children and students.

It is no longer the case (indeed it never was) that children go to school just to learn the three R's. They go to school with an infinite variety of needs and from an infinite variety of backgrounds. It is just as important to minister to the child's emotional needs as it is to teach him how to read and write as was so poignantly demonstrated in the case of Jena, who graduated with honors but ended up in a psychiatric ward. No matter how gifted, the emotionally troubled child or adult is usually hampered in regard to his own self-fulfillment and the contributions he can make to society.

While it is an awesome responsibility, the task of every teacher is to help each child grow intellectually, socially, morally and emotionally. Teachers do not teach math or English. They teach children. And whether they do so directly or indirectly, they do have a great impact on the lives of their students, socially, morally and emotionally as well as intellectually. The question as to whether teachers should have to assume responsibility in these areas or not is really not the question at all. The only real issue is that of direction. Will their influence be positive or negative?

As with teachers, many parents tend to shy away from their responsibilities in these areas, choosing instead to delegate responsibility to the school or church, believing they have met their obligations to their children if they provide a house, food, clothing and other physical and financial necessities of life. Whether by word or by action, parents, like teachers, cannot escape the influence they have on their children's lives, emotionally and otherwise.

Love

It has been said that love covers a multitude of sins. Although love is one of the most overused and abused words in our language, we cannot emphasize too strongly the importance of love and caring as the second prerequisite in the promotion of good mental health for children. Children at all ages desperately need and want support and nurturance from parents, teachers and other significant people in their lives.

Children are more resilient than we think. This resiliency becomes even more pronounced when the child feels loved. Most teachers and parents are conscientious and consequently prone to worry when they feel they have done something detrimental to the well-being of a child. But children can usually survive the many psychological mistakes we all make as teachers and parents, even profit from them if they are secure in the knowledge that they are loved and cared for by significant people in their lives. Most of the disciplinary problems and many of the learning problems in our schools and homes would disappear if these problem children felt they were genuinely loved by parents and teachers.

The previous statement is in no way intended as a blanket indictment of all teachers who have disciplinary problems in the classroom. Most do, though some have fewer than others. Many teachers with an abundance of love and affection to give are stifled in their attempts to do so by the child who is unwilling or unable to accept love. As with any love relationship, it takes two people willing to give and receive love before the relationship can be successful.

The most profound statement ever made about love was not made by a psychologist but is found in both the Old and New Testament—"Love thy neighbor as thyself." Five words, short and simple, but it is almost impossible to conceive of the changes which would occur in our society if this simple and direct command somehow could be implemented. If done, many of our psychiatric hospitals could be closed down as well as our munitions factories and military missile sites.

The command is not only good theology but good psychology, for it teaches not only love and respect for others, but for self as well. Unfortunately too many individuals have been led to believe that love of self is sinful. In so doing they fail to distinguish between conceit or selfishness and love and respect for one's self. Most prejudice and lack of respect for others is based on a lack of respect for one's self. The person who loves others probably has a healthy love of self.

Teachers and parents who are successful in creating a climate in the home or classroom in which the child is made to feel that he is both lovable and loving has gone a long way in laying the groundwork for a lifetime of good mental health.

Values

Many therapists, including such well-known psychiatrists as Viktor Frankl and psychologists such as Rollo May, are saying that more individuals than ever before are coming to their offices with the complaint that their lives are meaningless and lacking in purpose. We seem to be living in an age in which many of the traditional values and morals have been cast aside. The problem is that in too many cases they have not been replaced, thus leaving a void such as has never confronted mankind before.

Children need guidance. They need something to believe in and to hold onto with reasonable assurance that it will last. Despite the recent wave of permissiveness, children also need and want discipline. A child without discipline and values to guide him is like a ship without a rudder and will eventually suffer the same disaster.

It is impossible to live without values. Even therapists who go to great lengths not to influence their client's thinking admit that their personal values do enter into the relationship. In a similar vein, either by word or by action, parents and teachers communicate something of their personal values and beliefs to their children and students.

The wise parent or teacher encourages the exploration and development of a personal system of values for the child. They emphasize the virtues of commitment and dedication in life. This does not mean that all teachers should try to make Catholics or Baptists out of their students. (On the other hand, for many their religious beliefs may be a source of great meaning in life.) Nor does it mean that parents should insist that their children adhere strictly to everything parents hold dear. It does mean that children should be permitted to explore and think for themselves about the things in life which are important to them, and they should be encouraged to learn to make decisions and accept responsibility for their decisions when things go wrong. One of the saddest situations with which counselors are confronted is the older child or adult who has never learned to make a decision but still clings tenaciously to parental values with decisions still being made by mom or dad.

Communication

Like the word *love,* the term *communication* is tossed about with reckless abandon and with little meaning for most. Yet, in working with children and young people it becomes obvious that the inability of parents, teachers and children to communicate with each other is indeed a problem of major proportions.

As with love it takes at least two people before communication is possible. Unfortunately, too often parents and teachers see communication as a one-way street with the adult doing most of the talking. One of the major complaints heard from young people and children is that their parents and teachers never listen. The ability to listen seems for many a lost art but is in truth in many instances of greater value in opening the lines of communication and establishing dialogue with children than talking.

When it comes to listening it is surprising how many adults, who are supposedly interested and motivated, find it nigh impossible to attend class, church or some lecture and remain still and listen for even one hour. Yet, we expect children, during the most active time in their lives, to remain in their seats for six or seven hours each day listening to a history lecture or explanation of some math problem which they have little interest in hearing. Children need to feel involved. They need to feel that they are giving as well as getting.

The wise parent or teacher encourages involvement and expression of opinions, ideas and feelings as they occur. Even if they do not agree, it is important that children be heard and made to feel that their opinions and feelings are important with differences of opinion not viewed as an absence of love and respect.

Acceptance

In any discussion of human relationships it is important to distinguish between acceptance and tolerance. To tolerate something may mean that you put up with something even though you may dislike doing so. Acceptance, on the other hand, as we are using it in this context is more closely related to love and carries with it a healthy respect for the uniqueness of every child or student.

It is a tragedy that the uniqueness of individuals is too frequently sacrificed in our schools for assembly line techniques in which all children are treated as if they were the same.

As with schools which tend to turn out carbon copies of individuals rather than stressing individuality, parents often fall into the same trap. One of the most common mistakes made by parents is the comparison of siblings or comparison of their children with other children outside the family—"Why can't you be more like your older sister?" "Why don't you do as well in football as your cousin who was 'All State'?" How often children hear these or similar statements from parents and teachers!

The end result is that the child usually ends up feeling that he is not acceptable for what he is. Too often such children are made to feel that they can become worthwhile individuals only if they meet certain conditions laid down by parents and teachers. This does not lead to self-confidence, creativity, freedom of expression or the development of positive feelings about one's self as a unique person worthy of being loved unconditionally for what he or she is.

Praise

Everyone likes an occasional pat on the back. Recognition for a job well done can sometimes mean more than an increase in salary. Children especially need praise and encouragement. Unfortunately, too many parents and teachers believe the only way to motivate children is through the threat of punishment, scare tactics or criticism. This occurs despite the fact that it has been demonstrated again and again that children as well as adults respond more favorably to positive reinforcement than to negative.

One of the major problems encountered in counseling with college students is that of poor self-concept. In almost every case the beginning of such negative feelings can be traced back to either the home or the school. So often these students are heard to say, "I can never remember Dad praising me for anything I ever did," or "Mama was never satisfied with my grades. If I made a B she wanted to know why I didn't make an A," "My fourth grade teacher always picked me out to criticize before the class."

This is not to say that children should never be punished or criticized. It is to emphasize, however, how important recognition and praise are to children if they are to develop positive feelings about themselves. The child who receives adequate recognition and praise can learn to accept criticism in stride when it comes his way. On the other hand, the child who has never developed a strong image of himself due to constant criticism may fall apart when he is subjected to criticism in later years. The absence of praise may be interpreted by the child as a sign that he has failed.

Constant criticism may be seen as constant failure, and no human being can tolerate constant failure.

Identity

From the moment the baby emerges from its mother's womb it begins the long struggle for personal identity. The small child who insists on doing everything for himself is not being ornery; he is working toward the day when he will become independent.

While it is often difficult to do, the wise teacher or parent understands and supports this struggle for identity. It is important that parents and teachers recognize that the maturing child who is increasing in independence and establishing relationships outside the family is not being disloyal to his or her parents. Rather, the child is fulfilling the aim of effective parenting. He or she is becoming a person, an individual.

As the child grows into adolescence different degrees of rebellion will take place. This is in most cases the adolescent's way of asserting his self-hood. The wise parent and teacher knows how to tolerate the rebellion, disapproving when appropriate and giving latitude, provided the adolescent is not engaging in behavior unduly harmful to himself or to others.

In recent years we have heard much about the generation gap which troubles many parents. The truth is that the generation gap has always existed and always will. This is not only desirable but necessary. Parents have identities and needs quite different from those of their children, and the converse holds true. Thus, it is important that parents not see themselves as failures when the child refuses to adhere to all the values they have handed down. Rather than insisting that the child do so, it is important for the parents to know when to set limits and yet allow freedom for self-expression and development of the growing child.

As painful as the process of separation may be for both parent and child, it is essential if the child is to become a responsible adult in his own right. Recognizing this, the wise parent and teacher encourages the process rather than viewing it as proof that he has failed or that the child has turned out badly.

Time

A clergyman recently related an incident in which he had decided some years ago to take a holiday from his ministerial duties and take his small children on a trip to the mountains for a picnic. Although he did so he confessed that he was unable to enjoy himself for thinking about the sermon he needed to prepare and the hospital visits he needed to make. Later, even after he had retired for the night, he was still castigating himself for the frivolous way he had spent the day when so many more important things needed to be done. His wife's attempts to convince him that the children had enjoyed themselves did nothing to soothe his conscience.

Some years later when his children, now grown and in college, returned home for a weekend visit, he was surprised when he heard them talking of "the time Daddy took them on a picnic to the mountains." Although he had long since forgotten the event, they were heard to describe it in great detail as one of the most memorable days of their childhood, one of the few times they could remember in which their father had taken time off for a whole day to devote himself just to his family.

For too many parents and teachers, with their hectic pace and demanding schedules, time is the most difficult of all commodities to come by. Another of the most frequent complaints heard by counselors from children of all ages and backgrounds is, "My parents never spent any time with me." Children from affluent homes often accuse their parents of trying to buy their love by substituting gifts for time spent with their children. Teachers in overcrowded classrooms with untold housekeeping or administrative chores to perform freely admit that they seldom have time to give the needed attention to any child, especially those experiencing emotional or behavioral problems.

While there are some things beyond their power, most parents could recognize or budget their time to allow more time for their children. It is also important to remember that the quality of the time spent with childern is just as important if not more so than the quantity.

Caught up in the business of getting ahead or providing the

good life for our children, we often neglect the most important thing we have to give to our children and to our students—ourselves. Long after graduation the child will have forgotten most of the content of the teacher's lectures. He will remember as long as he lives, however, how much the teacher gave of himself to his students and the kind of relationship they had. Most adults cannot remember the kind of drapes Mom had in the living room or the color of the carpet in the house they grew up in, but they will remember with great clarity if they could go to her when things went wrong with the assurance that she would always take the time to listen.

Sensitivity

A young teacher having just completed his first year of teaching was heard to say that the most important lesson he had learned in his first year of working with ninth graders was the need to become more sensitive to the needs of his students. He then related how upset he had become when Frank, a sixteen-year-old-boy, went to sleep in his class almost every day for two weeks. Taking it as a personal insult and a reflection on his ability to hold the attention of the class, he had severely chastized Frank in front of the class.

Much to his chagrin he learned from another teacher the next day that Frank's father had been dead for almost a year. As a result Frank had been forced to go to work to help his widowed mother support his family which included three other brothers and sisters. He worked four hours each night cleaning up at a drive-in restaurant until midnight. He then got up at six each morning to help his younger brother deliver papers.

All behavior has a cause. We cannot always afford the luxury of knowing why people behave as they do, but as parents and teachers we should at least make an effort to discover the reason underlying behavior which we find disturbing in students and children. The parent or teacher who is sensitive enough and cares enough to take the time to listen and offer assistance to the troubled child may help avert a much more serious emotional crisis in the future.

Several years ago a story entitled "Cipher in the Snow" appeared

in the *National Education Association Journal* which, in our opinion, should be required reading for all teachers. This true and
prize-winning story, so eloquently written by Jean E. Mizer,
illustrates better than we ever could the point we are trying to
make. With permission it is reproduced in large part below.

It started with tragedy on a biting cold February morning. I was
driving behind the Milford Corners bus as I did most snowy mornings on the way to school. It veered and stopped short at the hotel,
which it had no business doing, and I was annoyed as I had to come
to an unexpected stop. A boy lurched out of the bus, reeled, stumbled,
and collapsed on the snowbank at the curb. The bus driver and I
reached him at the same moment. His thin, hollow face was white
even against the snow.

"He's dead,' the driver whispered.

... The driver looked down at the boy's still form. "He never even
said he felt bad," he muttered, "just tapped me on the shoulder and
said, real quiet, 'I'm sorry I have to get off at the hotel' That's all
Polite and apologizing like"

At school, the giggling, shuffling, morning noise quieted as the news
went down the halls. I passed a huddle of girls. "Who was it? Who
dropped dead on the way to school?" I heard one of them half-whis-
per.

"Don't know his name; some kid from Milford Corners," was the
reply.

It was like that in the faculty room and the principal's office. "I'd
appreciate your going out to tell the parents," the principal told me.

... "Why me?" I asked. "Wouldn't it be better if you did it?"

"I didn't know the boy," the principal admitted levelly. "And in
last year's sophomore personalities column I note that you were listed
as his favorite teacher."

I drove through the snow and cold down the bad road to the
Evans place and thought about the boy, Cliff Evans. His favorite
teacher! I thought. He hadn't spoken two words to me in two years!
I could see him in my mind's eye all right, sitting back there in the
last seat in my afternoon literature class. He came in the room by
himself. "Cliff Evans," I muttered to myself, "a boy who never
talked." I thought a minute. "A boy who never smiled. I never saw
him smile once."

... After school I sat in the office and stared blankly at the records
spread out before me. I was to close the file and write the obituary
for the school paper. The almost bare sheets masked the effort. Cliff
Evans, white, never legally adopted by stepfather, five young half-

brothers and sisters. These meager strands of information and the list of D grades were all the record had to offer.

Cliff Evans had silently come in the school door in the mornings and gone out the school door in the evenings, and that was all. He had never belonged to a club. He had never played on a team. He had never held an office. As far as I could tell, he had never done one happy noisy kid thing. He had never been anybody at all.

How do you go about making a boy into a zero? The grade school records showed me. The first and second grade teachers' annotations read, "sweet, shy child"; "timid but eager." Then the third grade note had opened the attack. Some teacher had written in a good firm hand, "Cliff won't talk. Uncooperative. Slow learner." The other academic sheep had followed with "dull"; "slow witted"; "low I.Q." They became correct. The boy's I.Q. score in the ninth grade was listed at 83. But his I.Q. in the third grade had been 106. The score didn't go under 100 until the seventh grade. Even shy, timid, sweet children have resilience. It takes time to break them.

I stomped to the typewriter and wrote a savage report pointing out what education had done to Cliff Evans. I slapped a copy on the principal's desk and another in the sad, dog-eared file. I banged the typewriter and slammed the file and cracked the door shut, but I didn't feel much better. A little boy kept walking after me, a little boy with a peaked, pale face; a skinny body in faded jeans; and big eyes that had looked and searched for a long time and then had become veiled.

I could guess how many times he'd been chosen last to play sides in a game, how many whispered child conversations had excluded him, how many times he hadn't been asked. I could see and hear the faces and voices that said over and over, "You're dumb. You're dumb. You're a nothing, Cliff Evans."

A child is a believing creature. Cliff undoubtedly believed them. Suddenly it seemed clear to me: When finally there was nothing left at all for Cliff Evans, he collapsed on a snowbank and went away. The doctor might list "heart failure" as the cause of death, but that wouldn't change my mind.

We couldn't find ten students in the school who had known Cliff well enough to attend the funeral as his friends. So the student body officers and a committee from the junior class went as a group to the church, being politely sad. I attended the services with them, and sat through it with a big lump of cold lead in my chest and a big resolve growing through me.

I've never forgotten Cliff Evans nor that resolve. He has been my challenge year after year, class after class. I look up and down the rows carefully each September at the unfamiliar faces. I look for veiled eyes or bodies scrouged into a seat in an alien world. "Look kids," I say silently, "I may not do anything else for you this year, but not one of you is going to come out of here thinking himself into a zero."

Most of the time — not always, but most of the time — I've succeeded.[13]

Fortunately many teacher-training programs now offer something in the way of sensitivity training. In our opinion such training should be required in an effort to make teachers more aware of the student and his or her needs as a total person. While it may be more difficult for parents, most who live in or near an urban area now have access to sensitivity or awareness training groups also. Many churches offer such programs in addition to those offered by university or mental health professionals in the community.

Consistency

It is important in working or living with children that parents and teachers provide an environment of behavioral expectations as consistent as possible. Where parents are concerned this involves the need to be consistent, not only as an individual parent relating to a child, but includes the need to be consistent with the other parents in the expectations communicated to the youngster.

The child who receives conflicting messages and expectations from Mom and Dad is apt to respond with conflict. The teacher who punishes the child for certain conduct one day and ignores it or finds it amusing the next is also displaying a lack of consistency so necessary if the child is to learn appropriate ways of responding to life's situations.

* * * * * * *

The precepts set forth above are clearly sketchy but nonetheless the core of a basic set of rules that offer the best chance of emotional self-fulfillment for the child and adolescent as well as for the parent and teacher.

Of lesser significance perhaps, but of varying degrees of importance, several other suggestions are offered regarding the creation of an environment by parents and teachers most conducive to the emotional well-being of children and students. They are as follows:

1. *Residence in a community for reasonable periods of time* (3 to 4 years). The emotional and social problems engendered by frequent moves are discussed in a book entitled *Corporate Wives—Corporate Casualties* by Robert Seidenber, M.D. The child who is forced to move about the country frequently, often ends up with feelings of rootlessness and instability. Such children frequently refuse to become involved in forming relationships in the new community since past experience has taught them that they will not be there long enough for a deeper relationship to evolve.

2. *Peer teaching and peer counseling.* Wherever shortage of teachers or counselors exist some amazing results have been noticed when children and adolescents are tutored or counseled by their peers. These techniques have been used, often unconsciously as a matter of expediency, in the one-room rural schools of years past. It is now even more obvious that when peers are used for tutoring or counseling in an organized and constructive fashion, the results are very positive for both the person doing the counseling or tutoring as well as the person receiving the help.

3. *Problem solving in the classroom.* This is simply the process of encouraging children to work together in the classroom, learning to solve problems rather than working in competition for grades. This strategy can involve academic as well as social and emotional problems brought up for discussion in the classroom. For example, rather than ridiculing or isolating the troubled child, the skilled teacher may develop a situation in which the class becomes involved in a learning situation for all in which ways can be explored to help the disturbed child. In so doing the troubled child is not only helped, but the class can learn to cope with situations of a similar sort sure to occur in other life situations. Children need to learn to deal with grief, anger and rejection as much as they need to learn how to add and subtract.

4. *Staffing of problem children.* This is the process in which

counselors, school psychologists, teachers and administrators involved with an emotionally troubled child come together to discuss the child. If necessary, outside professional consultants can be utilized.

5. *Frequent or periodic conferences with parents of all children.* Try to learn as much as possible about each child. Close cooperation between parents and teachers can often resolve problems before they become chronic or major ones. Even more frequent sessions may be called for with the child already emotionally disturbed.

6. *Child management training sessions to acquaint parents with the developmental needs of children and how to cope with them.* Such sessions are frequently conducted by community mental health professionals. Again, consultants outside the community may be of valuable service in this area. Such classes are gaining rapidly in popularity due to the emphasis on prevention of mental illness in recent years.

7. *More training for teachers in recognizing and working with emotionally troubled children.*

8. *Make school and home as pleasant and positive for the child as possible.* Schools can, for example, provide helpful and positive learning situations for the child preparing for life in the years ahead. On the other hand, teachers can also create an environment in which children learn to look at themselves, at others and at life in general in a most negative and unhealthy fashion. Unfortunately this too will affect greatly the way they approach life in the years ahead.

9. *Provide good role models as parents and teachers which children and students can identify with.*

10. *Recognize and work to overcome personal prejudices and inadequacies.* All human beings are biased and prejudiced in some way. Since parents and teachers do exert such great influence on children at such an impressionable age, however, it is important that they rid themselves of any feelings or attitudes which interfere with the development of a climate in which all individuals are given ample opportunity to grow toward self-actualization.

11. *Recognition of personal and emotional problems by teachers and parents.* Many parents and teachers are themselves emotionally troubled. It is disturbing to note, for example, the number of teachers who work with children who are in serious need of psychological help themselves. We are not referring here to the total absence of emotional problems as a prerequisite to teaching. If such were required, then none would teach. To be human is to have problems. Neither are we so much referring to the troubled teacher who has recognized the need for and obtained psychological help. We are more concerned with teachers or parents who are either unaware of emotional problems or who refuse to seek help even when they are aware of their personal need to do so.

Summary

As in previous chapters in which we have discussed the recognition of mental illness we have in this chapter once again directed our attention to parents and teachers regarding the promotion of good mental health in children and students. We have again done so as a result of our belief that parents and teachers constitute not only the two largest groups associated with children and young people, but because they also have the most influence in determining the type of environment children will be exposed to. While there are many differences in children, most children have two things in common if they live long enough—(1) most go to school in the morning and (2) most go home in the afternoon.

Since children and students spend a major portion of their time for the first two decades of their lives heavily involved in both home and school, it is only natural that it is here they develop attitudes and behaviors which they will use in large part for the rest of their lives. Assuming that most parents and teachers are interested in helping to provide a sound foundation for good mental health for children and students, it is believed that the implementation of some of the suggestions listed above in these most critical years will increase significantly the chances of most youngsters for a lifetime of emotional well-being.

Chapter 8

CONCLUSION

S OMEONE ONCE SAID, "When God wants something done He sends a baby into the world to do it." While the source of the quote escapes us, its impact does not. With apologies to the author if his intent is clouded by our poor memory or misinterpretation, we would like to think this was his way of expressing, among other things, the sanctity and worth of all children and the importance of their roles in life. We too feel that children are important and have their purposes in life.

Ideally we would hope to see the day when all problems and obstacles are eliminated which prevent children from realizing their potential or moving toward whatever it is they were created for or want to become. For some this may mean being a good mother or pursuing a career in medicine. For others it may mean finding God's purpose for their lives as singers or priests. For still others it may be the acquisition of personal wealth or political power or a million other varied interests and pursuits to which people dedicate themselves.

While we would not want it to appear that we see ourselves as being so omniscient as to tell others which road they should take, we do wish to stress how important it is for all children to be afforded every opportunity to discover for themselves the kind of life which will be most rewarding.

More realistically, however, we know that millions of children are prevented from achieving these goals for many reasons. In this book we have concerned ourselves primarily with what we believe to be one of the most formidable of the many obstacles which children have to overcome in their pursuit of a meaningful life. This major obstacle for many children presents itself in the form of mental or nervous disorders. Because of emotional problems, untold numbers of children and young people will never be able to enjoy or realize for themselves those things which make life most worthwhile.

We have undertaken to write this book because we believe most emphatically that a sizeable number of these children could overcome their emotional handicaps and experience a sense of self-fulfillment and personal achievement if these emotional roadblocks were discovered and help was provided early in life.

In attempting to smooth or eliminate some of the bumps or barricades on the road to better mental health for children we have attempted to recruit the two most potent groups in our society from the standpoint of numbers and influence—parents and teachers. We have done so with the hope that they will join forces in an effort to identify and obtain treatment for the potentially troubled child before the problems mushroom and become chronically debilitating.

In our search for recruits we are aware that the general public is appallingly apathetic whenever the issue of mental health is broached. Many are not only apathetic but downright hostile and negativistic. No later than yesterday, just prior to the writing of this chapter, we were told that a prominent educator had said, in discussing the funding of mental health programs in schools, that emotionally disturbed individuals should probably not be in school anyway. Granted, there may be isolated cases in which individuals may be too distraught to function in school, but for the most part such thinking displays not only colossal ignorance of mental health matters, but a most insensitive and callous attitude as well for the plight of millions who would be deprived of the right to an education if such thinking were to be applied on a large scale. No one would think of making such a statement regarding individuals afflicted with diabetes or heart disease. It is just such discrimination against the emotionally troubled as exemplified here, that makes our task to provide the much needed care and attention for emotionally troubled children a difficult one.

In addition, the thought of even talking to a psychiatrist or other mental health professional evokes unpleasant thoughts for many. While most people discuss quite freely physical health matters or problems, these same individuals are often reluctant to discuss their mental health.

This reluctance to discuss emotional concerns as compared to the ease with which physical health problems are shared with others is just another reflection of the archaic attitudes about mental health which still abound even in the latter part of the twentieth century. Patients visiting mental health agencies often go to great lengths to make sure none of their friends know they are going to see a shrink. We would like to see this attitude changed.

Even in the mental health profession itself it appears at times as if the term *mental* is a bad word, tinged with some sort of stigma and to be avoided at all costs. There is a noticeable trend away from the use of the term with many mental health agencies, deleting the word *mental* from their title, choosing instead to refer to themselves as growth centers, human development centers or some other title. Even the term *counseling* is now left out of the title of many agencies working with emotional problems in an attempt to entirely eliminate any possible inference that a person may be experiencing some sort of emotional conflict.

The attempt to change something perceived as undesirable into something more desirable through a change of title is not restricted to just the field of mental health. There seems to be a current fad in which numerous other groups or agencies have tried to change their images or statuses by changing their titles. Old people are now called senior citizens. Garbage collectors are called sanitation workers. Cemeteries are called memorial parks and barbers are referred to as hair stylists.

We are not opposed to such name-changing if it does indeed bring about a change in image or if it makes individuals feel better about themselves. However, in most cases the changing of names has done little to change the real situation or improve conditions. People are just as dead if they are buried in a memorial park as if they were buried in a graveyard or cemetery. Sanitation workers still pick up garbage, and senior citizens are still old people.

The tragedy is not in the failure of the name change to bring about drastic improvement. The real tragedy is that we think in such negative terms about mental health, old age or collecting garbage as a vocation in the first place. Rather than trying to escape something perceived as undesirable by changing the name, it is our position that far more positive results could be achieved if we exerted the same effort to change people's attitudes that there is something inherently bad about growing old, picking up garbage, cutting hair or seeing a psychiatrist.

The most outstanding example of the changes which can occur when a concerted effort is made to bring about change where deep-seated misperceptions exist is seen in the "black is beautiful" campaign in this country in the last decade. For years blacks were told that being black was something to be ashamed of. As a result, blacks tried to improve their lot by attempting to escape their blackness. Once they accepted being black as something beautiful, desirable and positive rather than something to be ashamed of and avoid, tremendous strides were made, both individually and collectively. For the first time, blacks are beginning to take their rightful place in our society and are viewing themselves as well as being viewed by others with respect.

While this is not a book on race relations, there is a lesson to be learned here by all people interested in changing attitudes about mental health and mental illness. This lesson has to do with pride rather than shame, sensitivity rather than apathy, involvement rather than avoidance, and enthusiasm rather than resignation.

If we can somehow, through a concerted effort on the part of parents and teachers, shift the emphasis from mental health as something negative, something to be dealt with in secret behind locked doors to a position in which we place the mental health of children on the same plane as intellectual and physical health concerns then we will have won a major victory. While there has been some change in the way individuals suffering from emotional problems are viewed by the public in recent years, there is still much to be done before the task of educating the masses is completed.

Our problem is further complicated by the lack of any really satisfactory definition of mental illness or mental health. As stated earlier, mental illness is in large part socially defined. Whether a person is considered mentally ill or not depends in large part on the time he is being observed and who is doing the observing and classifying. The truth is that mental health is on a continuum with all human beings falling somewhere from bad mental health to good mental health. There is no person who is totally insane any more than there is a person who is totally sane. All people referred to as insane do sane things, and all people referred to as sane do insane things. All human beings engage in behavior at times which would qualify them as emotionally disturbed if they behaved this way a major portion of the time. The person who had some weird dream last night in which she heard someone speaking who had been dead for ten years is the same person who, in her daily functioning, would never be thought of as mentally unbalanced.

The point we are trying to make here is that we are all both mentally healthy and mentally unhealthy in some ways. No one is in a position to cast stones. Rather than ostracizing people who seek psychological help we need to realize that the child or adult being seen weekly by a psychologist is not so different from the person who has never set foot in the offce of a psychiatrist or psychologist. To be human is to have emotional problems, and all people at times need help with emotional problems. The wise person seeks this help.

Summary

It is our hope that this book has in some small way made the reader more aware of the most serious health problem in this country today, perhaps in the world. It is also hoped that readers will not separate themselves into camps of we and they. We are all in this thing together. Emotionally we are all both healthy and unhealthy. Good mental health lies within the reach of most but in the ultimate sense is possessed by none. The person who prides himself on being strong enough to stand alone and handle all his problems may be more in need of help than the person who is seeing his psychiatrist weekly.

And, finally, we wish to reaffirm our position that children are our most precious assets. As such we believe they are deserving of the best we have to offer mentally as well as physically, socially, morally and intellectually. We would like to see the day when mental health is accorded its rightful place in our hierarchy of values. We believe these changes can come about if and when we can get enough people interested in children and their mental health.

Who knows, if we succeed, someday the mental health of our children may become as important as their test scores or even winning football games.

REFERENCES

1. Fitzgerald, F. Scott: *THE CRACK-UP.* Copyright 1936 by Esquire, Inc., Copyright 1945 by New Directions Publishing Corporation. Reprinted by permission of New Directions Publishing Corporation.
2. Barclay, Dolores: Killer kids inspire query: Whatever became of good old-fashioned juvenile delinquency? *The Brunswick News,* Brunswick, Ga., May 28, 1975, p. 1.
3. Freedman, Alfred: *Roche Report, Frontiers of Psychiatry,* Vol. 3, No. 18, Nutley, N.J., Nov. 1, 1973, p. 1.
4. Peterson, Karen: Pre-teens latch on to new kicks — alcohol. *The Atlanta Journal and The Atlanta Constitution,* Nov. 4, 1973, p. 21G.
5. Peterson, Karen: Pre-teens latch on to new kicks — alcohol. *The Atlanta Journal and The Atlanta Constitution,* Nov. 4, 1973, p. 21G.
6. Drugs link youth surge in suicides. *The Atlanta Journal,* Aug. 30, 1974, p. 1D.
7. Seabrook, Charles: Is troubled child neglected? *The Atlanta Journal and The Atlanta Constitution,* June 30, 1974, p. 1.
8. Couchman, Robert: Counseling the emotionally troubled: A neglected group. *Personnel and Guidance J, 52*(7):457, 1974.
9. Boroson, Warren and Rebecca: Eight warning signals that your child needs help. *Family Health V*(1):26-27, 42-44, 1973.
10. Couchman, Robert: Counseling the emotionally troubled: a neglected group. *Personnel and Guidance J, 52*(7):458, 1974. (Copyright, 1974, APGA. Reprinted with permission.)
11. Baird, Henry W.: *The Child With Convulsions,* New York, Grune, 1972, p. 10.
12. Gutgold, Margie: Ode to an anecdote. *The Personnel and Guidance J, 53*(7):500, 1975. (Copyright, 1975, APGA. Reprinted with permission.)
13. Mizer, Jean E.: Cipher in the snow. *National Education Association J, 53(8)*:8-10, 1964.

INDEX